PRAISE FOR I DECLARE WAR

"We are all created in the image of God. We don't have be chained by our feelings. We don't have to do the things we don't want to do. We don't have to be defined by our failures, mistakes, or sin. This is powerful! Yet how often do we not live based on this truth? One of the reasons I admire and respect Levi is his transparency and search for truth. He doesn't shy away from the hard or ugly stuff. Through his own story, he strives to help others get out of their own way and into the truth of who they are in God. This book will help you do just that!"

—**TIM TEBOW**, Heisman Trophy winner;
New York Times bestselling author

"As I read through the chapters of this book, each truth presented brought new freedom. As the chains of 'wrong thinking' clanked loudly on the ground, I barely noticed them as I marveled in the amazing joy and strength that 'right thinking' brought. All the doubts that you may have about reading this book are the very reason you need to. Take a stand for your future and read it."

—**STORMY** from California

"My friend Levi's new book could not come at a more important time. As we well know, anxiety, depression, and suicide are on the rise in our world today. In *I Declare War*, Levi gives us a field manual for the battles we face on a daily basis."

—**STEVEN FURTICK**, pastor, Elevation Church;
New York Times bestselling author

"I believe the message of *I Declare War* is inspired directly from God and will meet people where they are and apply to people in every walk of life. Levi's writing is humorous, thought provoking, and extremely relatable. I love the practical life steps that were given in this book to actively pursue life change."

—**LUKE** from Ontario

"Levi personally understands that the hardest battle is the one we're fighting against ourselves. That's why I'm so thankful he's poured out the biblical wisdom he's gained along the way into the pages of this book. The practical tools, scriptural teaching, and trusted guidance found in *I Declare War* are invaluable to anyone who wants to embrace victory in their own life!"

—**LYSA TERKEURST**, *New York Times* bestselling author; president of Proverbs 31 Ministries

"This book is for people who are tired of letting circumstances and personal habits control their lives. Spiritual warfare is not something to be taken lightly, and this book provides practical methods for not only engaging in this war but dominating in it. Levi Lusko is a much-needed voice for this generation. You absolutely have to read this book."

—**JORDAN** from North Carolina

"Gritty. Honest. On target. There is a battleground on which we all wage war every day: the minefield of our minds, hearts, and souls. 'I am my own worst enemy' is not just a catchphrase borrowed from pop culture but a spiritual reality that my friend Pastor Levi Lusko skillfully unveils in *I Declare War*. This resource is full of tools for your arsenal as you battle against the deceptive power of the flesh and for the beautiful things of God. Keep it nearby; your life, and eternity, depend on how you fight this battle!"

—**LOUIE GIGLIO**, pastor of Passion City Church; founder of Passion Conferences

"*I Declare War* is truly transformational. It lit a fire in me that won't soon be extinguished. This book has the power to change and influence an entire generation, and it definitely started with me."

—**RG** from Illinois

"A person's life is often a reflection of what they think about most. In turn, many of life's battles are won or lost in the mind. That's why Pastor Levi Lusko's new book, *I Declare War*, is one you will want to study and revisit regularly. In this powerful, practical book, Pastor Levi skillfully teaches us to capture our negative, anxious, fearful, jealous, and false thoughts—and replace them with God's truth. If your thoughts have been holding you back from God's purpose for your life, it's time to declare war."

—CRAIG GROESCHEL, senior pastor of Life. Church; *New York Times* bestselling author

"*I Declare War* spoke to my heart and mind powerfully and impacted me deeply. Packing countless hours of research, studies, scripture, and practical tools all into one place, this book helps equip every reader to be able to facilitate change in their lives and become the version of themselves they want to be. *I Declare War* is, hands down, one of my favorite books on this subject."

—DARIEN from Alberta

"I love this! Too many believers today are losing a personal battle that Jesus already won when he defeated death and the grave more than two thousand years ago. And he is right—declaring war over anxiety, fear, and depression is the right approach. This book is a must-read if you want more than just encouragement and one-liners. You will find practical help and actual steps to freedom from the very things that have their grip on you."

—JENTEZEN FRANKLIN, senior pastor, Free Chapel; *New York Times* bestselling author

"*I Declare War* is a battle cry for a generation that struggles with having free access to every bit of knowledge known to man and extreme anxiety about what to do with it. Levi gives us a clear battle cry to tackle our deepest demons and truly change the world."

—CASEY from North Carolina

"If you are content in your dysfunction and comfortable with your complacency, this book is not for you. *I Declare War* will not only expose your bad habits but will shake the foundations on which they stand. But if you are ready for radical change in your life, then open and study these pages. Cross the barbed wire fence. Declare war and see what a life uninhibited by dysfunctional behavior looks like."

—**ANDY STANLEY**, lead pastor, North Point Church; author, *Irresistible: Reclaiming the New that Jesus Unleashed for the World*

"Levi Lusko infuses scriptural truths, transparency, humor, relatability, encouragement, and tough love in order to mobilize readers to declare war on the version of themselves that they do not want to be. By learning to address their thoughts, feelings, and actions while simultaneously tapping into the power of the Holy Spirit, readers can expect a wolf to rise in their hearts in order to break the chains of sin and win the war within."

—**MORGAN** from Alabama

"Levi is someone I hand a microphone to in my life. What he says I want to be amplified. In *I Declare War* he not only is vulnerable with the struggles he has gone through and that we all have, but he equips us with scripture and weapons to bring an end to the battles you've been fighting all your life. This book will help lead us all to victory as we strive to go down in history as a healthy and strong generation."

—**SADIE ROBERTSON**, author of *Live Fearless*

"This book grips you in a way that inspires you to fight back. *I Declare War* is pivotal for everyone as arsenal against the enemy and the thoughts that block the life God has for you. This will be the book I recommend to every living person who comes my way facing a battle."

—**JESSE** from Texas

"Each encounter I've ever had with Levi Lusko has left me stronger and more encouraged. This new book promises to have the same impact on all who read it."

—MAX LUCADO, pastor and bestselling
author of *Unshakable Hope*

"Chapter after chapter I was hit with something that seemed to be exactly what I struggle with. At times, I was brought to tears because it hit home. This book is unlike any other. It grabs you with its ability to relate to so much of your life; then it helps you realize how to win the war against the evil one."

—HAILEY from Kentucky

"*I Declare War* is a deeply powerful challenge to elevate the truth of Scripture above any circumstance or challenge you may face so that you can claim the victory already won for you by Jesus. Levi's personal story of fighting back the darkness will encourage you as you fight back your own."

—CHRISTINE CAINE, bestselling author;
founder, A21 & Propel Women

"I can confidently say that throughout this book I started to feel hope again. Reading this has allowed me to break down and process what I need to do in order to declare not just war but eventual *victory* over my thoughts and mind."

—MARISA from Colorado

"Levi is a gifted communicator who carries a heartfelt determination to help every person step into their God-given potential. He is full of faith and is unafraid to engage with relevant issues in order to point people toward the truth of God's Word. I know his teachings will greatly encourage you and help you rise to live with compelling victory in Christ."

—BRIAN HOUSTON, global senior pastor,
Hillsong Church

I Declare War

ALSO BY LEVI LUSKO

Through the Eyes of a Lion: Facing Impossible Pain, Finding Incredible Power

Swipe Right: The Life-and-Death Power of Sex and Romance

I Declare War

4 KEYS TO WINNING
THE BATTLE WITH YOURSELF

LEVI LUSKO

W Publishing Group

An Imprint of Thomas Nelson

Published in Nashville, Tennessee, by W Publishing, an imprint of Thomas Nelson.

Published in association with the literary agency of Wolgemuth & Associates, Inc.

Thomas Nelson titles may be purchased in bulk for educational, business, fund-raising, or sales promotional use. For information, please e-mail SpecialMarkets@ThomasNelson.com.

ISBN 978-0-7852-2086-2 (TP)
ISBN 978-0-7852-2087-9 (eBook)

Library of Congress Cataloging-in-Publication Data
Library of Congress Control Number: 2018907009

Printed in the United States of America
19 20 21 22 LSC 10 9 8 7 6 5 4

To every family member, friend, coworker, and stranger who has had unpleasant encounters with the version of me that I don't want to be.

CONTENTS

CARD 4: PHANTOM POWER
(THE HELP YOU NEED TO WIN THIS WAR)

Introduction

WHEN THE WOLF RISES

*To be prepared for war is one of the most
effectual means of preserving peace.*

George Washington

There is nothing I can do to stop it.

My stomach flutters, and my skin is glistening with sweat. Thinking about all the different ways I could possibly die by my own hands, I lurch from sleep with a sickening quickness, like an unbuckled crash test dummy in a simulated collision. My mind races, and my eyes burn. The voice in my head telling me I am going to kill myself sounds like me, but it is not on my side. Helplessly I watch myself moving toward a path of self-harm—and I have no emergency brake to pull. Panicking, disoriented, and scared, I stumble out of bed and pace the hall, trying to figure out where I am and why I am so afraid.

Under my breath, I mumble a trusted Bible verse from my arsenal over and over. (Hang with me until the end, and I will let you look at the weapons I keep in my war chest for specific situations just like this.) Eventually I'm able to bring down my mind's RPM from a scream to a dull roar. The fear that hung in the air like a thick, acrid smoke soon dissipates, and I start to feel like things will be all right. I peel my T-shirt and towel off my damp skin before crawling back into bed.

Variations of this 2:00 a.m. ritual have played out as far back as I can remember. On the worst nights, my sheets are so covered in sweat that I have to lay down a towel before I can try to drift back to sleep. (If I'm staying in a hotel by myself, I just switch to the other side of the bed.) At one point in my youth, these episodes got so bad I literally retched with fear. My parents vividly recall praying over me.

The Bible calls these fits "terror by night" (Psalm 91:5), and in the moment it feels like being locked in a maze with no exits. I don't always have suicidal thoughts; sometimes I fear harm happening to my children or making a mistake with enormous, terrible implications. For many years my fear took the form of a sense of pressure and urgency, as though I were forced to figure out a puzzle underwater, in the dark, in a language I didn't speak, with the weight of the world bearing down on me and a thousand loved ones' lives depending on my ability to do what I knew I couldn't. There was a period when the fear mostly involved sermons I had written that in my sleep seemed to be terrible. Don't even get me started on the dreams involving snakes.

Fortunately, the sleepwalking has mostly stopped. It was pretty bad for the first twenty-five years of my life. Once, when

I was a child, my mom found me standing over our cat's litter box, and when she asked me what I was doing, I told her I needed to go to the bathroom.

"Not in here, you're not," she shot back as she grabbed my shoulders and directed me to the bathroom. My eyes were open, but I didn't know what was happening.

On an overseas trip I woke up by the vending and ice machines down past the elevators—in my boxer shorts. I had to convince the front desk person to give me a key before I could get back into my room. Another time I woke up in the hotel hallway and assumed I was locked out, but when I plunged my hands into my robe's pockets I found a key card at the bottom. I mouthed a quick thank-you to sleep-walking Levi and went back to my room. And then there was the time I jumped out of my seat on an airplane backward because an Indiana Jones–size boulder was coming toward me. I ended up in the lap of the very surprised person in the seat behind me and apologized with the sheepish explanation, "I was having a bad dream."

The night terrors haven't gone away, but I have learned how to manage them better. They seem to ramp up when something big is about to happen, like when I'm facing a major opportunity or when our church is about to expand.

Unfortunately, nighttime isn't the only time my mind locks up with fear; daytime can be just as scary. Anxious thoughts, fears, worries, and the regrets that come when walking away from a conversation you wish you could do over—all can be just as difficult.

Sometimes I watch myself shifting slowly into a funk that I know will lead to unhappiness. I become like Bruce Willis in *The Sixth Sense*. I try to avoid this well-worn path that leads to nowhere. I plead with myself, *Turn around! Quit pouting. This is not the way to get what you want. Use your words and stop sulking!* But I don't seem to heed the warning, no matter how much I wave my arms and raise my voice.

This is not even to mention the addictive way I mindlessly turn to social media, online shopping, and other digital distractions when I am feeling sad, lonely, unappreciated, or bored, or when I am just avoiding working on something great. Oh, yeah—I also look to food to give me comfort when I am down. Carbs are my go-to agent for a quick hit of happiness when I am blue. The empty calories never seem to fill the emptiness in me that I am trying to shove them into, and I know I will feel worse in half an hour, but that doesn't stop me from shoveling chips into my mouth by the handful.

I don't know if you can relate to my issues. Maybe you've never had to towel down in the middle of the night as though you've just finished an Orange Theory workout in your sleep, or ended up in a hotel lobby in your underwear, but I have a feeling you probably have some situations that you don't have an answer for, something that makes you feel terrified, trapped, lonely, victimized by your own bad behavior. Maybe you're numbing yourself with something you download or a substance you drink—a medication to dull the pain—and it's starting to scare you. You used to turn to it to feel good but now you need it just to feel normal. Perhaps it's a cycle of retaliation with your spouse that leads to a vicious silence that no one is willing to break—and if something doesn't change, your marriage isn't going to last. Perhaps you're ready to quit your job because all your coworkers and your boss are against you, just like at the last three places you worked and the last three churches you left and the last three friends you ended up estranged from. Maybe it's your temper. You haven't crossed the line and actually hit someone, but you've come close.

Bad moods by day, or bad dreams by night. You have problems you feel unable to do anything about. Debilitating fear in a crowded room or crippling anxiety when you wake up alone. The worst thing about being victimized is that it's impossible to be a victim and a victor at the same time.

That's why I decided to declare war, and I want you to join me.

I have no doubt that the devil sends demons to mess with me, and the world might very well be another source of problems that come at me. But this I know for sure: I cause more than enough problems to keep myself occupied. The three sources of my primary frustration in life are as follows: me, myself, and I. I am my biggest enemy, and I desperately want and need to get out of my own way.

So I declare war: On darkness. On my demons. On anxiety and succumbing to the nights of the black dog of depression. On my self-sabotaging tendencies. My selfishness. My narcissism and the way I can spend hours doing nothing when I should be focusing on only one thing.

I declare war.

I am not asking you to help me fight my battles, but I want to do everything I can to convince you to engage with yours.

I declare war.

There is such power in those three words. Say them out loud slowly, focusing on each of the four syllables: *I / De / Clare / War.*

There is freedom in this declaration.

You can't win a conflict you don't admit you are in.

Declaring war separates you from the problems that you can so easily mistake for permanent parts of your identity and distances you from your thoughts, your fears, and your anxieties. You are not your dysfunctional behavior. You are not your overeating, or your obsessive TV watching, or your judgmental, critical comments you wish didn't keep coming out of your mouth. You are not your mistakes or your transgressions or what you see in your dark and twisted dreams. Choosing to oppose those things is to make it clear that they are not on your side. This is the only way to get out of your rut and move past them.

When you choose to declare war, you are refusing to go gently in the night or to be taken without a fight. You are declaring war on the version of yourself that you don't want to be.

CROSSING THE BARBED WIRE

When you decide you're done playing the blame game and you're ready to become a victor, you will find that a wolf rises in your heart. That is how Theodore Roosevelt, the youngest person to hold the office of president, described the "power of joy in battle" that floods a person who chooses to meet the challenge spread out before him. This larger-than-life president, who is literally chiseled in stone on Mount Rushmore (and is permanently one and the same with Robin Williams because of *Night at the Museum*, at least in my mind), led the Rough Riders on horseback into the battle for San Juan Hill

YOU ARE DECLARING WAR ON THE VERSION OF YOURSELF THAT YOU DON'T WANT TO BE

during the Spanish-American War. Mauser machine gun bullets sprayed out from the top of the mountain, cutting down man after man, yet Teddy fought on, relentlessly urging his men forward.

In that terrible situation he crossed a barbed wire fence that lay on the battlefield and fully committed to the action before him—and at that moment a wolf rose in his heart. With his trademark spectacles fogged up from the humidity, and a handkerchief trailing from the back of his sombrero, he gave no thought to the bullets flying all around him as he urged his horse, Little Texas, forward. (His other horse had drowned while being unloaded from the Navy transport that dropped them on the island.) Teddy had flipped a switch inside, and he was unstoppable in his resolve to do what was necessary. A witness said that from the instant he stepped across the wire he "became the most magnificent soldier I have ever seen." A shell exploded near him, burning his skin, yet he pressed on. A stray bullet nicked his elbow, but he didn't notice. He didn't stop until the battle was won. For the rest of his life, he referred to that day, July 1, 1898, as the greatest day of his life.

I am not saying you need to go to Cuba to fight. I am saying there is incredible power in setting all that is within you in a singular direction. So much of the time, we defensively react to what comes our way. Stop letting life happen to you, and start happening to your life. Meet the enemy on your terms. Go on the offensive. Whether you are a sophomore in college or are in your sixties and contemplating life after retirement, when you decide to stare the things in the face that are holding you back, a strength will bubble up inside your chest. As twentieth-century Scottish explorer W. H. Murray wrote, "The moment one definitely commits oneself, then Providence moves too . . . raising in one's favour all manner of unforeseen incidents and meetings and material assistance, which no man could have dreamt would have come his way."

Declare war, and the wolf will rise. Don't overthink it—you have time to work through all the implications. And you're not going to have to fight alone; you have an enormous amount of backup and firepower at your disposal. I'll tell you all about it.

This book will help you discover the keys to winning the battle within yourself. I've divided it into four sections, one for each syllable of the statement *I / De / Clare / War* (just like in the card game War we played as kids). Each section, or card, deals with a vital component of your internal struggles. And each card builds toward the most vital card—the fourth one.

It is essential you make it to the end. As good as the first three cards are, they won't matter without the all-important fourth card.

I have lived the principles I'm going to share with you. They're at play in my life right now, as I sit here in this coffee shop in Sioux Falls, South Dakota, writing this book on my iPad. Every manner of distraction, depression, and gloom has filled my mind the past few months as I prepared to write. But I finally crossed the barbed wire because I know you need these concepts as much as I do.

Before you move on to the first card, on the next page, write down your declaration of war. In what ways do you need to get out of your own way? Don't sanitize your list. The time for half measures is over. To be clean, you must come clean.

THE THINGS HOLDING ME BACK

_____

_____

_____

_____

I DECLARE WAR

ON THIS DAY _____

AT THIS TIME _____

SIGNED _____

1 ♥

DECLARE
WAR ON

WHAT YOU THINK
YOUR THOUGHT LIFE IMPACTS ALL OF YOUR LIFE

♠ 1

THE WOLF YOU NEVER
KNEW YOU WANTED TO BE

*I want to be alone and I want people to
notice me—both at the same time.*

—Thom Yorke of Radiohead

In Las Vegas, the escalators and moving sidewalks seem to move in only one direction: toward the casinos. Getting in is as easy as finding a Ding Dong in a truck stop. On the other hand, finding your way out is, by design, much more difficult. The intention is to trap you in a maze of distraction that will cause you to spend as much time and money as possible.

When I find myself struggling with moodiness, I feel as though I'm being carried along on a moving sidewalk, headed to a place I won't like and that I'll have a hard time finding my way back from. I started experiencing this sensation in high school. Something would happen to set me off: feeling excluded, being made fun of, embarrassing myself with something I said or did. The next thing I knew, I felt like the ground was moving under my feet.

There was almost always a moment of clarity when I knew I was at a crossroads. In the direction I was heading, I could see storm clouds brewing, vultures circling, the bones of bleached wildebeests that had been picked clean shining in the last moments of sun. This is where my moving sidewalk was taking me, and I hated it.

In the other direction I would see Candy Land—vivid colors, warm light. People smiling and jumping rope, explosions of joy radiating across their faces. If I wanted to be where they were, I would have to make a decision and make it fast, because each moment that passed took me further away from the village of joy. If I did nothing, I would be taken straight to the badlands of gloom.

More often than not, I just stood there. Eventually the movement would end, and I would be left in a world of gray too far from the color to see it, with no idea how to get back.

I was officially in a bad mood. Well, some people call it a *bad mood*. I call it *being held hostage by the version of me I don't want to be*. You can rearrange my name to spell *evil*, so I call him *Evilevi*. He might have my fingerprints and blood type, but he is no friend of mine.

Whether it set in after lunch, during second period, or in the car on the way to school, once I was in it, I was *in it*. A wall went up, and my enjoyment of life went down. It's impossible to be at ease when you're clenched up on the inside. After an hour or two, whatever originally set me off was no longer the issue; self-pity and self-loathing were the real problems, and

SOME PEOPLE
CALL IT A

BAD
MOOD

I CALL IT BEING

HELD
HOSTAGE

BY THE VERSION OF ME
I DON'T WANT TO BE

they hardened into a mask I felt unable to remove. Eventually I'd give up on the entire day. I'd get to a place where I'd think, *This day is spoiled. I'll just have to try again tomorrow.*

You've felt that way, haven't you? As though so much of the day has been wasted that there's no use trying to make good decisions. *Tomorrow is a new day. This one's no good.* We do the same thing when we've made a bad choice about eating: *I fell off the wagon for lunch, so I might as well binge at dinner and have a cupcake at bedtime. I should have had a healthy breakfast, but since I didn't the whole day is shot. I'll do better on Monday . . . or next month.*

Where did we get the idea that one bad decision must be followed by another? Maybe it comes from failing to understand the true meaning of an often-quoted verse written by the prophet Jeremiah in the book of Lamentations:

> Because of the LORD's great love we are not consumed,
>> for his compassions never fail.
> They are new every morning;
>> great is your faithfulness. (3:22–23 NIV)

What a Bible verse *doesn't* mean is as important as what it *does*. Jeremiah isn't saying that a new morning is the only time you have the opportunity to receive mercy; there isn't anything mystical attached to the clock striking midnight. That's not when God's mercies replenish. Your AT&T data plan might roll over at a specific time, but that's not so with the devotion God has allocated for you.

Rather, what Jeremiah emphasizes is that you always have a new shot—because *God is that good.* You have the option to go to him morning, noon, and night—once a day, nine times a day, every hour if you need to—and claim the help you need for the present struggle you are facing. Hebrews 4:16 says, "So let us boldly approach God's throne of grace. Then we will receive mercy. We will find grace to help us when we need it" (NIrV). You don't have to wait for the start of day; you can seek the grace when you need it.

Astronauts on the International Space Station orbit Earth every ninety minutes, which means they can watch the sun rise and set sixteen times a day. Why? Because they're moving quickly around the earth. How quickly? My friend Shane Kimbrough, who has spent 189 days in space and was the commander of the ISS, told me that when you're on the space station, you are moving 17,500 miles an hour, or 5 miles per second, 200 to 250 miles above the surface of the earth. The picture of an astronaut sitting in the Cupola, watching the sun rise and set sixteen times in one day through the enormous window, is key for you to remember as you lean in to the reset God wants to give you: as the heavens are high above the earth, so God's ways are past finding out (Isaiah 55:9; Romans 11:33). The higher you go the more sun rises there are. You needn't write off a day that has been tainted. You can start over on the spot. Shake your internal Etch A Sketch! There are brand new mercies waiting for you. Only pride and silliness allow a bad decision to turn into a bad day and make you defer until tomorrow what you need to do right now.

I love the convenience of calling for an Uber. (I always say "*call* an Uber." I know you don't *literally* call them, but I don't have any intention of stopping.) A few clicks of a button, and a car shows up where you are, ready to take you wherever you need to go. It's Amazon Prime for traveling across town.

Quite a few times I have mistaken a vehicle coming to get me with a car on its way to get someone else. Once at an airport I hopped into the back seat of the Uber I had ordered only to discover it wasn't an Uber at all. The driver was even more surprised than I was! The truth is, you don't have to stay in a bad mood any more than you have to stay in the wrong Uber. If you got in, you can get out.

Smells Like Teen Spirit

A bad mood exists only in your mind. That's why the first of the four cards to set down when you declare war deals with your thoughts. You can't live right if you won't think right.

My senior year, I had art class last period. The class was in a metal barrack on the far end of campus. A gravel path snaked past the cafeteria and gym, the sagging chain link fences, and the area where buses picked students up before winding its way to a row of portable buildings. It has been seventeen years since I was a seventeen-year-old making my way from sixth to seventh period, but I can still hear the gravel crunching under my feet and feel the weight of my backpack loaded up with books. (Whether I would crack them open that evening was another story.)

I can vividly recall how it felt to walk to art class in a bad mood. It happened regularly enough that I haven't forgotten those angsty feelings churned up by near-lethal doses of self-loathing and self-pity.

My shirt was usually untucked. We had uniforms at my high school—you had to wear a polo shirt or an oxford button-down with khaki or navy pants. You received a write-up if you were caught with your shirt not tucked in. I usually had it tucked in only above my belt buckle—just enough to claim it wasn't technically totally untucked. What a rebel.

Sometimes a friend who could see the funk on my face would walk with me and ask what the matter was or how my day was, and I'd shove down my emotions and lie through my teeth. "Everything is fine," I would say, even though inside I wanted to admit it wasn't.

Luckily the day was almost over. *Maybe tomorrow will be better. This day is doomed.*

The funny thing is that, even though I can remember walking to art class in a bad mood, I can't recall a single occasion when I walked out of art class grumpy, angry, or wound up.

We each had a little cubby where we would paint, draw, sketch, or color for forty-five minutes. My teacher was a kind woman named Mrs. Losey, and on occasion she allowed us to bring in music to listen to while we worked. I'd slip the headphones of my Discman over my ears, press play on a worship music CD, and fill blank pages with lines, colors, and shapes. Before I knew it I was shuffling back on that same gravel road but in a completely altered state. Miraculously, the spell had lifted, and the funk I had been in less than an hour ago was gone.

I didn't have the self-awareness to realize then what I understand now: it wasn't coincidence that I was in a different emotional place by the end of the period. That art class was like the calming phrase used to soothe the Hulk's rage and transform him back into mild-mannered Bruce Banner: "The sun is getting real low, big guy" (when Black Widow said it, not Thor). The combination of music, art, and the quiet place were a lullaby that took me to a completely different headspace. My heart rate dropped, and with it my levels of cortisol, the hormone that wreaks havoc on your system when you're stressed. It was as though the bad mood was a six of clubs, and the music and art were the king of hearts. And no numbered card of emotions can overcome Jesus—the King of your heart!

I've learned a lot about what makes me tick, but I still struggle to control my mood. My ability to respond well to external battles has everything to do with my ability to fight the internal war successfully. I'm reminded of Joshua fighting the Amalekites while Moses stood on the mountain above the battle, raising his arms with the rod of God in his hands (Exodus 17:8–13). It didn't matter how much effort Joshua expended; when Moses' arms sagged, Joshua lost momentum, and when his arms were steadfast, the tide turned. Hear me loud and clear. Nothing so influences your life as your ability to control your spirit in the midst of volatile feelings and the madness of life.

Proverbs 25:28 tells us, "Whoever has no rule over his own spirit is like a city broken down, without walls." In the ancient world, walls were everything. A city without walls was the equivalent of a hotel room without a lock, deadbolt, spy hole, or flippy thingamajiggy that lets a door be opened a couple inches. You wouldn't feel secure in your hotel knowing you were completely vulnerable to invasion. That's why Nehemiah's crusade to restore the walls of Jerusalem was so important. When we neglect to control our spirits, we leave them vulnerable to attack.

When God created Adam and Eve, he sculpted their bodies

NOTHING SO
INFLUENCES YOUR LIFE
— AS YOUR —
ABILITY
TO
CONTROL
— YOUR —
SPIRIT
IN THE MIDST OF
VOLATILE
FEELINGS
— AND THE —
MADNESS OF LIFE

from the dust with his fingers, but it was his breath that gave them their spirits. Your spirit is the part of your being that responds to God and receives his power.

The word *spirit* shows up hundreds and hundreds of times throughout Scripture. Here are some of the highlights:

- When you are saved, your spirit is the part of you that is most affected: "I will give you a new heart and put a new spirit within you; I will take the heart of stone out of your flesh and give you a heart of flesh" (Ezekiel 36:26).
- When you sin, your spirit gets off kilter and needs recalibration, like a compass near a magnetic field: "Create in me a clean heart, O God, and renew a right spirit within me" (Psalm 51:10 ESV).
- You must learn how to control your spirit, and then practice doing so, especially in times of anger: "He who is slow to anger is better than the mighty, and he who rules his spirit than he who takes a city" (Proverbs 16:32).
- Your spirit can have good intentions, but it can be overcome by sinful desires and needs to be fortified by prayer: "Watch and pray, lest you enter into temptation. The spirit indeed is willing, but the flesh is weak" (Mark 14:38).
- A calm spirit causes you to have a quiet confidence: "He who has knowledge spares his words, And a man of understanding is of a calm spirit" (Proverbs 17:27).
- We can ask God for a spirit marked by generosity just like his: "Restore to me the joy of Your salvation, and uphold me by Your generous Spirit" (Psalm 51:12).
- An extraordinary spirit leads to open doors and promotion: "Daniel became distinguished above all the other

high officials and satraps, because an excellent spirit was in him. And the king planned to set him over the whole kingdom" (Daniel 6:3 ESV).

- God is drawn to those who have a spirit marked by humility and those who lift their eyes to him when in pain: "The LORD is near to those who have a broken heart, and saves such as have a contrite spirit" (Psalm 34:18).

Learning how to steer your spirit by managing your thoughts is incredibly important. *If your spirit is out of control, it's difficult to put your life under God's control.* And a spirit under God's control is key to the wolf rising in your heart.

Hold on! I can hear you objecting. *About that . . . I'm not really sure I want to rise up like a wolf. In the Bible, aren't wolves described in a negative light?* Not to mention all the fairy tales—even Little Red Riding Hood and the three little pigs know that wolves are big and bad.

Thank you for bringing that up. How like the devil to want to completely own the image of an animal with attributes we desperately need. Yes, the enemy does attack us like a wolf, but he also likes to dress up as an angel of light, a serpent, and a roaring lion. We don't seem to have any problem appreciating angels and lions, and Jesus told us specifically to be wise like serpents. So why would we write wolves off? If anything, the enemy's interest in them should tip you off that there is something powerful about them.

Wolves were created by God and are truly remarkable creatures—known for loyalty and strength. In addition to being highly social and smart, they also have other lesser-known qualities you should want in your life. They have been scientifically proven to be susceptible to contagious yawning (did you yawn when you read that?), which is believed to be linked to empathy. And this is my favorite: wolves are very rare in that they're willing to adopt orphaned wolf pups even if they belong to a rival. Among apex predators this is not normal. Even lions (and I have a lot of love for lions) who take over another pride will almost always practice infanticide, killing all the lion cubs to end the blood line of their predecessor. But not wolves. The new alpha male and alpha female will tenderly care for the pups of their enemy and bring them into their pack. How touching is that? It's a bit of a cliché to speak of someone with bad manners as having been "raised by wolves," like Mowgli the man-cub. But there is some truth behind this expression, as these ferocious hunters also willingly play the part of foster parents.

Read this excerpt from *The Wisdom of Wolves* and tell me if you don't find yourself wanting to channel your inner wolf:

> They care for their pups with a familiar devotion and share our reflexive instinct to care for youngsters, related or not. They hold a place in society for their elders. They push boundaries and explore, then return to visit their families. They care what happens to one another, they miss each other when they're separated, and they grieve when one among them dies. . . . They are benevolent leaders and faithful lieutenants, fierce mothers, nurturing fathers, and devoted brothers; they are hunters, adventurers, comedians, and caregivers.

To be a wolf is not just to be a brave warrior; it is also to be a loving nurturer, and that is your destiny.

Back to the story in Exodus 17. Moses eventually grew exhausted, and try as he might, he couldn't keep his arms in the air. Luckily, his friends Aaron and Hur improvised a couple of hacks: they stuck a rock under Moses like an old-school bar stool, and they stood by his side and each held up one of his arms. Moses was in the exact same position he had been in before, only now it was much easier to keep his arms raised.

We can be creative in involving the help of other people and even props to keep our spirits in check. This is true whether your struggle is losing your temper with your kids, interacting with a rude or condescending customer service person, or dealing with an unprepared coworker. Or, in my case, seeing someone on our team yawning or showing no enthusiasm in a preservice huddle. (My Hulk side flashes to life on this one.) Something as simple as where you sit, what you bring with you, or the way you prepare yourself for a complex encounter can be the difference between a controlled response and a response you will regret. For example, I heard of one person who brings water with him into conversations where he knows he will be tempted to lose his cool. Before shooting off his mouth, he takes a sip. No one blinks an eye at someone drinking instead of talking.

I leave you with three takeaways from this chapter: First, no matter how much of the day has been spent, it's not too late to change course—not tomorrow, but right now. Second, having a name for the version of you that you don't want to be helps you call yourself out when you're behaving badly. Decide a name for your own version of Evilevi. Once you have a name for your alter ego, you can take them off the guest list. Name that version of you before it claims you. Third, you don't have to go to Mrs. Losey's art class to calm yourself down. New mercies are only a prayer, a breath, a short walk, or even a sip of water away. Slip your ear buds in. Throw a song on. Close your eyes for a little bit. Buy a small set of watercolors to keep with you. Figure out what your equivalent of art class is so that you can hit reset on what you believe you are stuck inside. Escaping your self-imposed hostage situation might not be as easy as hopping on the moving sidewalk that brought you there, but that's okay—you can take the stairs.

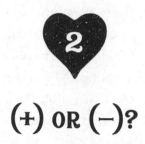

(+) OR (−)?

*Whether you believe you can do a
thing or not, you are right.*

—ATTRIBUTED TO HENRY FORD

My kids love to play with the dome lights in the car. There is something satisfying about the way a dome light clicks on and off, so I completely understand the urge. My wife and I have tried to instill an awareness of the need for these lights to be turned off before they get out of the car, but this doesn't always go as well as we would hope. So it was no surprise when Jennie told me her car battery was dead.

I'm always looking for an excuse to feel like a manly man, so I valiantly told Jennie, "No problem. I've got this!" Then I said to my oldest daughter, Alivia, "Come help Dad jump Mom's car" and motioned toward the garage as though I were Tim "the Toolman" Taylor.

I popped the hoods of both cars. "We're going to use the life from my car to send life to Mom's," I explained. But Alivia looked at me quizzically when I told her that the next step was to find the snaky things with the metal teeth. (Granted, that's probably not how your average automotive shop describes jumper cables.)

Unfazed by her rapidly deteriorating level of childlike amazement, I carefully connected the cable to both batteries. "Being careful is key, especially after the live battery is hooked up," I told Alivia. "Because if the teeth of the two clips touch once you have juice flowing, well . . . you got a one-way ticket to sparky town, baby. *Sparky. Town.* Been there, done that, don't want to go back."

Once I'd started my car, I asked Livy to get behind the wheel of Jennie's and fire it up. "Livy, hit it."

Nothing.

"I said, hit it."

Nothing.

"Righty-tighty, baby, righty-tighty."

"Um, Dad? Is the garage supposed to be full of so much smoke?"

"Just turn it again, honey . . . Wait, what smoke?" I asked as her question finally hit my brain a full five seconds later.

"Daddy, the jumper cables are melting!" she cried.

I shot out of my car. Sure enough, the jumper cables *were* melting, like the faces of the Nazis in *Raiders of the Lost Ark*. Burnt rubber dripped all over the cars, all over the ground, forming a puddle made up of liquefied black and red cable.

The smart thing would have been to turn off my car, or to tell Alivia to run for help, but I didn't know what to do. I just stood there, watching in disbelief.

Soon the rubber melted away, leaving just a wire holding the two jumper cables. Then the wire fell to the ground, leaving only jumper, no cable. I stared at the clips attached to the two batteries, at which point I noticed that I had a red (positive) clamp connected to a black (negative) terminal and a black clamp connected to a red terminal. I slapped my forehead and explained to Alivia what I had done wrong.

Afterward, when I told the story at church, someone explained that I'd made a dangerous mistake. The reversal of polarity can cause a buildup of hydrogen gas within the battery that can ignite or explode. Also, the heat that melted the insulation on the cables was hot enough to solder with and could have created a surge powerful enough to permanently damage all the electronics that modern vehicles depend on.

Great. I had basically made a homemade hydrogen bomb and had come unwittingly close to unleashing an EMP. Fortunately no one was hurt, and I was able to clean up the melted plastic without leaving any on the car or the garage floor. After we found a second set of jumper cables, I was able to start both cars without incident.

Here's the takeaway lesson: bad things happen when you put a negative where there is supposed to be a positive. This isn't just good car battery advice; the same is true when it comes to your mind. If you put a negative thought where there should be a positive one, you won't blow up, but you won't grow up into the version of yourself that you want to be.

I have known a lot of people in the church who sneer at the idea of positive thinking, as though it were somehow a betrayal of the gospel. It seems to be one of those things some Christians love to bash (along with global warming, secular music, and evolution). A while back I realized that, almost without fail, those who are quick to look down their noses at the power of positive thinking and view it as a carnal and unspiritual thing also happen to be pretty negative people. This much I know for sure: the more I've paid attention to the "polarity" of my mind, the more I've liked the direction of my life.

Don't misunderstand me: I don't believe in positive thinking as a replacement for God but as a response to God. My goal isn't that you would see your metaphorical cup as half full; I want you to see it as constantly overflowing! What is faith if not a filter that allows you to process your experiences through the goodness of God, choosing to reject what you see and clinging to what you trust he is doing? Faith allows you to believe your beliefs and doubt your doubts.

Is it possible to replace Jesus with positivity? Yes. But everything that makes your soul better carries that danger. You can do church without Jesus. You can pray without praying. You can give all you have to the poor and have it count for nothing. Just because something can be done the wrong way doesn't mean it isn't ever right.

Positive thinking isn't evil; in fact, you will see just the opposite in Scripture. It's not offensive to God; it's obedience to him. The shortest verse in the Bible makes that crystal clear: "Rejoice always" (1 Thessalonians 5:16).

Wait a minute, you might be thinking, especially if you grew up in church and did Bible sword drills like I did at VBS. *The shortest verse in the Bible is John 11:35: "Jesus wept!" That's only nine letters, compared to the thirteen letters in the verse from 1 Thessalonians.*

I DON'T BELIEVE
— IN —
POSITIVE
THINKING
— AS A —
REPLACEMENT
FOR GOD
BUT AS A
— RESPONSE —
TO GOD

That's true—in English. But the Bible wasn't written in English. It was written in Hebrew, Greek, and Aramaic. And in the original Greek, "Jesus wept" is sixteen characters, and "Rejoice always" is only fourteen, making it the shortest verse. Pow.

But don't let its size fool you; this little guy packs a punch. It is both powerful and challenging.

Personally, I think that this tiny, little, two-word-long verse is one of the most difficult things we are told to do in all of Scripture. Rejoice *always*? Think about that: not some of the time or when things are going great, but *always*.

Paul tells us specifically that ever-present joy is a part of God's plan for our lives: "Rejoice always, pray without ceasing, in everything give thanks; for *this is the will of God in Christ Jesus for you*" (1 Thessalonians 5:16–18, emphasis added).

Why is it important to God that you rejoice all the time, pray frequently, and stay thankful? Because it is impossible to do those things and be negative at the same time. When you feel like complaining, see yourself acting selfishly, or find yourself slipping into a bad mood, shoot a prayer to God that is full of joy and gratitude instead. Setting your mind on things above you is declaring war on low-level thinking.

The fact that it is God's will for you that you be positive doesn't make it easy. It was such a struggle for me when I was young that my dad nicknamed me "Mr. Negative." Having a negative mind-set was responsible for so much of the moodiness I experienced in high school, and to this day, it's still a battle for me to be positive.

If you let negativity in the door, it will want a seat at the table—and if you give it a seat at the table, it will want to sleep in your bed. (Basically, feeding Mr. Negative is like giving a mouse a cookie or a moose a muffin.) Soon negativity becomes your default mode.

I heard someone say his mother became so set in her negativity that one day he called her and said, "Hey, Mom, it's October 1 today." And she responded, "I know. Isn't it dreadful?" What a stunning lack of positivity for no apparent reason! The reward for gloominess is more gloominess.

Fortunately for you and me, we are not alone in our struggle. Despite his prolific, mountain-moving faith, the famous evangelist and America's pastor Billy Graham had a hard time in his private life dealing with negativity. I found this description reassuring:

> Billy's faith was more of a "faith despite." His children state that the possible problems and difficulties always came to his mind first. Because of that, they teasingly called him "Puddleglum." Puddleglum is a character from the fantasy series the Chronicles of Narnia by C.S. Lewis. As a born pessimist, Puddleglum always has a dark view of things. Just like Puddleglum, Graham tended to see the glass half empty instead of half full. But when Graham was active on the spiritual front, he was a completely different person. He was full of faith, and nothing could deter him from the goal of proclaiming the gospel under all circumstances. When it rained cats and dogs during a mission, he would walk up to the microphone, request everyone to be quiet, and then pray to God to make a dry hole above them, and the rain would stop, as it happened, for example, at a mission in 1997.

Did you catch that? In his ministry, he had no problem brazenly commanding the rain to stop. But it was hard for him to shoo away the cloud over his own head.

One of his coworkers said being around Billy in ministry was an uplifting experience: "Some people low-rate you. They pull you down. You become downtrodden and depressed in their presence. Billy is exactly the opposite. The radiance of Christ exudes from his person and being with him is a blessing." But he admitted that there were moments when it was better to leave Billy alone. Especially at home, Billy had to lean on his wife's positive disposition.

Billy wasn't alone in swinging between the highs of optimism and the lows of pessimism. Throughout Scripture, we see need for the wolf to rise in the battle against negativity—a battle that seems to be particularly prevalent among those who, like Reverend Graham, are eminently gifted and used in extraordinary ways.

Ups and Downs

Elijah certainly understood what it felt like to crash from the highest of highs to the lowest of lows. He went up solo on Mount Carmel against 450 prophets of Baal in a contest to see whose god was real; the god that answered with fire would be the winner. The prophets of Baal danced and sang, jumped and spun, cut themselves until blood gushed out, but Baal was silent.

Elijah mocked them relentlessly. I can imagine his taunts: *Maybe Baal's hearing aid is turned off! Perhaps he's on the commode, and you will have to shout louder.*

Eventually the prophets gave up, exhausted. Elijah repaired the broken altar and prepared his sacrifice. But then he did something strange: he ordered the Israelites to douse the sacrifice with twelve barrels of water.

If I had been one of the Israelites, I would have objected. If you want to start a fire, soaking it is not a great plan. *Wet wood doesn't burn!*

Dousing the sacrifice is significant for two reasons: First, God can do the impossible, and he often calls us to do the impractical. He regularly asks people to do things that seem odd and then blesses them supernaturally. He likes to stack the deck against himself so that he receives all the glory. *Wet wood is not a problem.* In fact, where God is concerned, the wetter the better.

Second, it's important to know that the Israelites were facing a three-year-long drought. The water they poured out must have come from their personal water supply. What they'd been told to give up was the very thing they needed more of. Elijah knew that as long as they had any water remaining, they would depend on it, but in pouring out all they had at his feet, they were in essence putting their faith entirely in God.

Elijah calmly took his place. There would be no shrieking or hysterical writhing. He never cut himself. All he did was pray a simple prayer so short it could have been tweeted before tweets could have 240 characters: "Hear me, O LORD, hear me, that this people may know that You are the LORD God, and that You have turned their hearts back to You again" (1 Kings 18:37).

At that moment, fire fell from heaven and consumed all the meat, all the water, all the wood, and even the rocks. *Hello!*

Elijah then ordered all 450 false prophets be brought down to the valley to be executed. (The job of a pastor sure has changed over the years.)

It was an amazing moment—and God wasn't done yet. Elijah prayed for the rain to return, sending a servant out seven times to see if the prayer had been answered. Eventually a pathetic little cloud the size of a man's hand showed up, but that little cloud soon filled the sky and drenched the earth. The Israelites got their twelve barrels of water back and then some. It's beautiful, isn't it? The water they had poured out was turned to steam by God's fire; then it rose to heaven, where God multiplied it and returned it as much more than what was given. The seed never looks like the harvest it contains.

With the nation rejoicing in water, and the evil prophets of Baal dead, you would think Elijah would be excited. He'd just thrown an eighty-yard, game-winning touchdown pass in the Super Bowl, for crying out loud! But that's not how his story goes. He entered into a funk that almost took him out. Despite the fact that all Israel was looking to put him on their shoulders and sing, "For he's a jolly good fellow," Queen Jezebel posted on her Facebook page that she was going to kill him, and it sent him on a downward spiral of negativity and sadness that completely demolished the good spirits he was in on Mount Carmel. It was a total buzzkill.

He crashed so low that he ended up running a hundred miles away—as far south as he could go. He plopped down under a broom tree and prayed that he might die: "It is enough! Now, LORD, take my life, for I am no better than my fathers!" (1 Kings 19:4). The highest high was followed by the lowest low.

Jonah, too, had an up-and-down ministry. He gets a lot of

flak for his whole running-from-God thing—though to be fair, if we understood how insanely wicked the Ninevites were, we'd cut him more slack. These guys would pile up the skulls of their victims outside their homes as decorations. They would remove lips and noses and treat them as badges. They would cut off people's eyelids and tie them outside in the sun so that they had no way to blink or turn their gaze away from the burning ball of gas that would permanently blind them, turning their eyeballs into raisins. So I get that when God sent Jonah to preach to them, he ran the other way.

What impresses me is that he eventually came around and agreed to go. Sure, it took an extended trip to SeaWorld; so what if he had to become sushi in reverse—a raw human eaten by a fish? He eventually preached the gospel to one of the most bloodthirsty civilizations ever, and the entire nation repented. It was such a revival that everyone from the king to the peasant clothed themselves in sackcloth and ashes to reveal their remorse and penitence. They even put sackcloth and ashes on their animals. Can you imagine that? People's dogs and cats were getting saved!

It is likely that this was one of the largest responses to a preacher's messages in human history. But Jonah, like Elijah before him, sank into a slough of despair that made him want to die.

Paul could definitely relate to this struggle. The same guy who wrote thirteen out of twenty-seven books of the New Testament was a tortured genius, and he wrote in Romans 7 an honest, relatable articulation of the reality of being your own worst enemy: "I am not practicing what I would like to do, but I am doing the very thing I hate. . . . Wretched man that I am!" (vv. 15, 24 NASB). He realized he had created his own demons.

Charles Swindoll wrote, "I'm glad that when God paints the portraits of His men and women, He paints them warts and all. He doesn't ignore their weaknesses or hide their frailties." Amen! Elijah's, Jonah's, and Paul's struggles were just as real as yours. You are not alone in your battle to keep your mind from drifting into negativity. And this battle isn't going anywhere. If you think, *I can't wait until I mature so this won't be an issue anymore*, you're setting yourself up for disappointment. There is truth to the expression "new levels, new devils." If anything, the battle grows more complex as you progress in your spiritual journey, because the more you do, the more the enemy will try to stop you.

Plan for the Worst, Hope for the Best

I have been preaching for twenty-one years—full-time for fifteen—and I wish I could tell you that winning this battle is a piece of cake. But in truth, so often my mind is a bag of cats. And one of the reoccurring problems that drags me down is a reversal of the polarity—from positive to negative—that God wants for my mind.

It is so important that we nail this concept down right now, because your words (card 2) and actions (card 3) both begin as thoughts. To quote a great line from the cinematic masterpiece *Kung Fu Panda 3*, "Before battle of fist must come battle of mind." Listen to me carefully: negative thoughts can't lead to a positive life. You probably never wake up and think, *I want to have a bad day* or *I want to be a bummer to be around* or *I want to suck the joy out of people I encounter*. But we all have allowed ourselves to think the kinds of thoughts that lead to a negative day.

That means you can change the way you feel, by changing the way you think. I'm not talking about ignoring your emotions or pretending you don't feel a certain way but rather letting God give you a new perspective. Your feelings are real, but they are not the boss of you.

I'm not advocating for a fluffy, self-help type of positive thinking in which you naively believe that because you tell yourself everything is going to be fine, it automatically will be. Remember, this isn't a glass half-full type of optimism; that's much too small. I am talking about a life-to-the-full positivity. It's true that you have a God who anoints your head with oil, causes goodness and mercy to follow you all the days of your life, and prepares a table for you (Psalm 23:5–6). But let's remember that the table he is preparing for you is located in the presence of your enemies—which presupposes that you have enemies.

And you do. Internally, externally, spiritually, professionally, relationally. People will oppose you if you are on the right track. We tend to ask, what did I do wrong? But the better question would be, what did I do *right*?

Victor Hugo wrote, "You have enemies? Why, it is the story of every man who has done a great deed or created a new idea." No one gets to live his or her dream without other people trying to turn it into a nightmare. Opposition is table stakes for living the life you were born to live. Of course, there is an easy way to make the critics go away: do nothing, contribute nothing, stand for nothing, *be* nothing. When you live out your calling, you will always face potshots from people who have given up on theirs.

NEGATIVE THOUGHTS CAN'T LEAD *TO A* POSITIVE LIFE

Jesus actually said, "Woe to you when all men speak *well* of you" (Luke 6:26, emphasis added). That goes against our obsession with pleasing people, but you can't please God and man at the same time. Of course people will try to take a bite out of you when you dare to do something great—for many of them it will be the only taste of greatness they will ever have!

Factor opposition into your positive thinking. Plan on stuff going wrong. I give a monthly talk to our staff at Fresh Life. One recurring theme is an ongoing list I call "Because I am a leader," in which I offer various confessions. One that made the list recently was "I am not surprised by setbacks. I antici- pate them, am energized by them, and have a plan to deal with them." That's the kind of powerful positive thinking that won't be devoured by the brutality of life and the regularity of plans going awry. It teaches you to reframe how you see the hard- ships you face and not be caught off guard by them. Instead, you can say, "What's taken you so long? I've been expecting you." You can't be blindsided by what you are prepared for. You can predict obstacles and setbacks and prepare the steps you will take to deal with them when they arise. Come up with contingencies and backups. If you fail to plan, you are planning to fail.

At this point in my life, I would be concerned if we were preparing for a major initiative or outreach at Fresh Life and something *didn't* go haywire. The opening lines of *A Tale of Two Cities* often prove true of all major breakthroughs: "It was the best of times, it was the worst of times." No one told me when I was young that the two often go hand in hand.

Anticipating obstacles and being prepared for them helps you reframe the story you write in your head in the midst of challenging seasons. In the book *Extreme Ownership: How US Navy SEALs Lead and Win,* the authors, two former Navy SEALs, tell of a phrase that they have made a ritual. No matter what happens to them in the midst of all manner of madness coming their way, they choose to think in response, *Good times.* Regardless of how unexpected, inopportune, or inconvenient the task in front of them, they allow themselves only the response of *Good times.* They trust the plan and each other, which gives them confidence and assurance in moving forward. That response puts them in the proper frame of mind to stay strong and increases their effectiveness. In essence, they are taking a potentially negative situation and seeing it from a different perspective. Instead of "bad" they are calling it "good." Psychologists call this tactic *cognitive restructuring.* It allows them then to be on their toes and not on their heels as they move forward.

I dare you to try it.

Dishwasher broken? *Good. Now I'll get some time to think and listen to a podcast while I wash dishes by hand.*

It's raining again? *Good. I love the smell of rain.*

They're out of pumpkin cream cheese muffins at Starbucks? *Good. That's forty-five burpees I don't have to do!*

The company is cutting back on hours? *Good. I have dreamed for a long time of figuring out a way to make money online, and now I have the push to make it happen.*

I realize you might be pushing back on this. While it makes sense for rainy days and when appliances go down, it doesn't feel big enough to counter the horrible hardships you have been through.

I feel you. But the way to use the word *good* that will cause the wolf to rise in your heart isn't to say that the bad thing is good—but to believe that goodness will be the end result. Your pain is just a scene; it's not the entire movie. It's a chapter, not the book. David, a Navy SEAL of the Old Testament, focused on goodness this way when he wrote, "I would have lost heart, unless I had believed that I would see the *goodness* of the LORD in the land of the living" (Psalm 27:13, emphasis added).

What kept Joseph bright eyed and bushy tailed when his flesh and blood turned on him, his boss's wife made false sexual allegations about him, and people he helped broke their promises and forgot to return the favor? It was holding on to hope that God was working all things together for good. And at the end of the day, that is precisely how his story turned out. He declared over his hardships, "You meant evil against me, but God meant it for *good*" (Genesis 50:20, emphasis added).

Job suffered like few ever will. Yet God had a plan, and that plan was good.

The ultimate goodness of God's plans is what was on Paul's heart when he instructed the Thessalonians, "Rejoice always, pray without ceasing, *in everything* give thanks; for this is the will of God in Christ Jesus for you" (1 Thessalonians 5:16–18, emphasis added).

Did you catch that? He didn't say to be thankful *for* everything. You aren't supposed to be thankful for death or divorce or unemployment. Those things aren't good. You can, however, be thankful *in* those things—or in any other thing hell can throw at you—because God has a plan to produce good from what you are facing.

When I'm bummed, I think of this poem I once came across in a devotional:

Would we know that the major chords were sweet,
  If there were no minor key?
Would the painter's work be fair to our eyes,
  Without shade on land or sea?
Should we know the meaning of happiness,
  Should we feel that the day was bright,
If we'd never known what it was to grieve,
  Nor gazed on the dark of night?

Many men owe the grandeur of their lives to their tremendous difficulties.

Jump-start Your Mind

I was recently walking through Costco and saw something I knew would change my life. (No, it wasn't a churro—though I do love a good churro.) It was a mobile battery jumping device. The size of a backup phone battery, it had a cord with two little alligator clips to attach to a dead car battery so you can jump it without the use of another car. All you have to do is charge it via a USB cord; then it can be stashed in the glove box until you need it.

I instantly knew this was something the Lusko family needed. It reduces the risk of confusing polarity and it's portable. That means that no matter where Jennie or I go, we could have juice. No flagging down a stranger, no having to push a car into position so another could nose up to it. A portable jumper device meant freedom.

Think of your ability to reverse your polarity through

gratitude, prayer, and thanksgiving that way. You'll never be stranded. You don't have to wait for anyone to show up and rescue you. Just open the glove box to access a portable power source that is with you wherever you go. You don't need anything else to get the dead battery of your thoughts roaring again; you just need to flip your mind from negative to positive.

Levi, you might be thinking, *this isn't rocket science; it's common sense*. Exactly! The simplicity is what creates complexity. In life the things that are easy to do are also easy not to do. It's remarkably simple to lose weight—eat fewer calories than you burn—and yet more than two-thirds of Americans are overweight or obese. Becoming rich shouldn't be hard—you just need to spend less than you earn. Why is it, then, that we are the most in-debt generation in history?

Knowing what to do and doing it is not the same thing. They don't call it a mind-set for no reason. You have to set your mind. Give it a try. It'll work. I'm positive.

3

TSA ON THE BRAIN

Perfection is finally attained not when there
is no longer anything to add, but when there
is no longer anything to take away.

—Antoine de Saint Exupéry

Chapter 2 was a caution; this chapter is the solution. Now that I've told you the dangers of being negative, I want to talk to you about the how of being positive. You will make fewer wrong decisions when you are thinking the right thoughts. You can't live right if you don't think right.

It's been said that you shouldn't ask a question if you don't want to know the answer. The same is true of looking for things that you don't want to find. For example, when going through security at the airport, don't look too carefully at the bin you put your belongings into.

On a recent trip, I glanced down into the tray where I was

YOU WILL
MAKE
FEWER
WRONG
DECISIONS
WHEN
YOU ARE
THINKING
THE RIGHT
THOUGHTS

about to place my belt, phone, and wallet, and realized there was a long, black hair in the bottom.

I am a full-grown adult, and such things shouldn't bother me. It bothered me.

What is it about a strand of hair that is so disgusting? You ever notice how ten seconds after a hair leaves your body, you completely turn your back on it? It's been with you its entire life, but the moment you notice that it is now on a bar of soap or the shower wall instead of growing out of you, you treat it with contempt.

I have absolutely no room in my life for someone else's hair. I took my contents out of the bin as fast as I could and grabbed a new one, but it, too, had a hair in it.

What shedding pack of wooly mammoths had traveled through this airport?

By now people were piling up behind me, so I waved them through. I was determined to find a follicle-free receptacle. After my fourth bin and my fourth stray hair—this one curly, vomit!—I set my stuff inside bin number 5, which finally passed my visual inspection. But when I was retrieving my items on the other side of the X-ray machine I saw it: a little hair not longer than an inch, winking at me like a giant eyelash. Careful not to touch it, I shuddered, grabbed my things, and made my way to my gate in defeat.

A hundred flights and a hundred hairs later, it dawned on me: there are hairs in every bin. *Every last one.* Check next time you fly. They are *all* hairy. Trust me. Some hairs are blonde, some are black; all of them haunt my dreams. Once I realized this, I resolved never to look closely in a TSA bin again. Some questions are better left unasked.

Now when I travel I grab a bin from the stack, turn it upside down, and give it a smack before placing my belongings inside. My hope is that whatever stowaway tresses trying to smuggle themselves home in my bag will be shaken loose. Is that little ritual enough to overcome the static field that makes these dirty communal plastic pieces such a haven for hiding hair? I don't care. The placebo effect is fine by me.

If you ever see me in a TSA line and it seems like I'm not focusing my eyes, it's not because I'm high or hungover—I'm just trying not to see all the hair Chewbacca left in my bin. As long as I don't take a closer look, I'm not bothered by what I can't see.

That brings up what I want to talk to you about. (No, not hair; that was simply an opportunity to get some free therapy, since Jennie and the girls won't listen to me complain about the subject anymore.) I want to talk to you about TSA and why you need to install checkpoints in your mind.

In battle, the advantage always goes to the side in control of elevated positions. That's why it was so important for the British to displace the American patriots in the Battle of Bunker Hill, for the Allies to take Normandy from the Axis powers, for the United States to beat Russia in the space race, and for Elon Musk to get us to Mars.

It is critical that you realize that your mind is the high ground of your life. In *Paradise Lost*, John Milton observed, "The mind is its own place, and in it self / Can make a Heav'n of Hell, a Hell of Heav'n."

When I taught my daughter Alivia to snowboard, one of the most important things I tried to get her to understand was that where she turned her head would determine where her body would go. So if she wanted to set up a turn to her heel edge, she needed to look over her left shoulder. To turn to her toe edge, she needed to look over her right shoulder. Otherwise, all the footwork in the world would be in vain. Your body is really good at following the direction you face.

That is why you need a TSA-style checkpoint in your skull. TSA wields such power; they are in total control of what you bring onto the plane. Once you step up to the podium and hand over your documents for inspection, you are totally at their mercy. Accidentally bring fireworks with you? They're not getting through. Bring a six-ounce bottle of shampoo in your carry-on? Kiss it goodbye. Sayonara, bear spray you forgot you had in your duffle. You have to do whatever the TSA agents tell you to do and can only bring beyond the checkpoint what they deem is safe for you to have with you.

And if you ever forget your ID, you will discover the lengths these agents will go to as they carry out their job. One time I was flying through Newark, New Jersey, with only a temporary driver's license, one of those paper ones the DMV prints out on the spot when your real one is coming later in the mail. For whatever reason, it wasn't a problem on my outbound segment, but in Newark, the agent didn't recognize the temporary ID as valid. He pulled me off to the side and explained that he would have to do a thorough examination of my person and possessions.

By thorough, I was soon to do discover, he meant he had to slide the back of his hand over every square inch of my body. I have been married for thirteen years, but this screening involved places my wife doesn't even know about.

The guy was a total pro about it. He even gave me a cigarette afterward. (I'm joking.)

I know this sounds like a rant about the screening process,

but it's actually a recommendation for *more* screenings in your life, not fewer. You should go through TSA every time you do anything—but I want *you* to be the TSA agent. (You even get to wear the badge.) Imagine installing in your mind one of those check-in stations, an X-ray machine, and even one of those hands-in-the-air, feet-on-the-footprints scanners. So before you let your cerebrum get a Cinnabon and plop into a chair at gate E17, you need to force your thoughts to go through inspection.

And you are . . . ?

Boarding documents?

Maybe you should add a customs agent to the routine, as long as you are at it.

Purpose of your trip? How long do you intend to stay in the country?

Not only do you have the permission to screen your thoughts, the Bible explicitly commands you to: "Finally, brethren, whatever things are true, whatever things are noble, whatever things are just, whatever things are pure, whatever things are lovely, whatever things are of good report, if there is any virtue and if there is anything praiseworthy—meditate on these things" (Philippians 4:8). Paul recommended that you have a filter in your head—a screening process that you pass thoughts through before you let them come in and make themselves comfortable. *Are you true? Well . . . not really. Sorry, you are denied entry. Are you noble? Obviously not. How about pure? Yeah, you're not getting in here. Would you be described as lovely? Definitely not. Buh-bye.*

I love the last part of that verse as it is rendered in *The Message*: only allow into your mind "the best, not the worst; the beautiful, not the ugly; things to praise, not things to curse."

Can you even imagine how much of a game changer it would be if, as you drove the kids to soccer, did laundry, walked to third period, led a staff meeting, ran on the treadmill, or waited to fall asleep, you allowed into your mind "only the best, not the worst; the beautiful, not the ugly"? Would you even recognize the peace-filled person you had become?

A study back in the 1980s revealed that people have on average 500 intrusive thoughts every 16 hours, each lasting an average of 14 seconds. Many of these intrusions are just worries or anxious thoughts; 18 percent are mean, unacceptable, or politically incorrect—and 13 percent are ugly or downright shocking: shoving a stranger off the subway platform, running over a pedestrian, stabbing a partner, raping or strangling someone, smothering an elderly parent, or driving your car off a bridge.

That amounts to 116 minutes a day of some sort of unwanted, unwelcome, unhelpful thoughts stealing our joy and neutralizing our effectiveness.

To be clear, the problem isn't that these thoughts show up. The problem is that we let them pull out the sofa bed and spend the night. An old saying warns us that you can't stop birds from flying around your head, but you don't have to let them build a nest in your hair.

This is why it is so essential to install a checkpoint in your mind. Without such a filter, you risk two hours of thoughts sneaking through and causing untold amounts of terror and damage to your peace and your God-given power. When you force each thought to go through this screening before you allow it to remain, you can take back control from fear, shame, jealousy, guilt, and doubt.

You'll find that being so alert to what you're thinking will have a huge impact on your emotions. Remember, you can change the way you feel by changing the way you think. Where the head goes the body must follow.

I am a big baby and also a control freak. When things aren't going my way or when my plans are being changed or misunderstood, I find myself bristling. I feel like a bird whose feathers are being rubbed the wrong direction. I sense Evilevi rising. But when I remember to put those negative thoughts through the scanner, I can clearly see that I am thinking only about myself. If I take the time to articulate why I'm unhappy and what is causing me to act out (yelling at my kids, being short with my wife, being overly harsh with someone at work, or being mad at a complete stranger who I think is being a jerk), I can trace those actions to feelings, and the feelings back to thoughts I never should have allowed in my head in the first place.

Think about a time you did something you regretted: cutting off someone while driving, sending a mean text, chewing someone out. (If you can't think of anything, feel free to borrow an example from my life; I have an abundance of mistakes for you to work with.) Now think of the feelings you were having that lead to that decision. Behind those feelings were probably thoughts that didn't belong.

I Choo-choo-choose You

I love visiting New York City. It's like no other place on earth. The buzz is contagious, and you can't help but feel your heart quicken just being there. I love waking up early and walking the streets of SoHo before things get humming. New York might be the city that never sleeps, but on the weekends, it is definitely the city that sleeps in. If you get up at the right time, you can have the place virtually to yourself. Watching the sunrise while walking the cobblestone streets in solitude is spectacular.

Despite the many times I have been to New York, I am still an absolute amateur at navigating the subway. Complete rookie noob status times ten thousand. Even if I can figure out which train I need to take, I absolutely stink at figuring out which side of the street to enter the subway platform from, which has everything to do with whether the train is heading uptown or downtown. More times than I care to admit, I have gotten on the subway going the opposite direction I need to go. The feeling of the little lights on the subway map moving in the wrong direction is the worst.

My friend Kevin Gerald likes to say that "thoughts are like trains—they take you somewhere." When a train of thought shows up, don't just get on! Slow down before you board it to make sure it's heading in the right direction. Ask each one: *Where are you taking me? Are we headed to Lovelyville, Virtuetown, Good Report Station? Boomsauce! Wait, this train is going to Jealousy, USA? Rage City? Gossip Central? I'm sorry, I'm just not comfortable going where you are headed. Unlike Lisa Simpson, I don't choo-choo choose you!*

This is an obvious strategy when you're staring down a shocking or a perverted thought. Thoughts of murder, for example, can pretty quickly be spotted as trains you don't want to get on. But you can also avoid boarding trains like these:

- *You'll never top this success; you've peaked.*
- *You'll never escape your past.*
- *You'll never achieve your dreams.*

- *You'll never make it out of this alive.*
- *You don't have what it takes.*
- *You won't get to see your kids grow up.*
- *You're defined by the difficult things you have been through.*
- *You don't deserve anything good.*
- *Nobody loves you, and you should just die.*

Sometimes, though, it's harder to spot trains headed to negative destinations. Watch out for thoughts like these:

- being suspicious of people's motives
- wondering what went wrong
- feeling guilty
- doubting and questioning God
- worrying
- obsessing about why you weren't invited
- fearing someone you love being harmed
- secretly being happy when something bad happens to someone you don't like
- stressing about your future
- stewing over something that was done to you

The point is, you have a choice.

Throw It in the Pit of Despair

You can avoid a train that's headed to a dangerous destination by not boarding it in the first place. What do you do when you identify a thought that doesn't pass inspection?

The same thing TSA would do if the X-ray machine showed a weapon in your carry-on: you take it captive. Detain it. Don't let it in to your mind for a minute. Show it no mercy. Give it no quarter. Send that thought to the pit of despair so the six-fingered man and the albino can torture it.

Don't be kind. Remember, this is war.

This is the time for the wolf to rise in your heart. As Teddy Roosevelt himself put it, "Better a thousand times err on the side of over-readiness to fight than to err on the side of tame submission to injury, or cold-blooded indifference to the misery of the oppressed." I put my daughters in boxing lessons because I want them to speak softly *and* carry a savage left hook. You need to be the one with the left hook when your thoughts are oppressing you and making you miserable.

You can't stop thinking about something by trying to stop thinking about it. The only way not to think about pink elephants is to instead think about something else. You have to feed the positive and replace the negative.

You don't turn off darkness by yelling at it, waving it away, or willing it to be gone; you walk across the room and flip the light switch. (Or you ask Alexa to turn the lights on.)

Never look where you don't want to go. Don't focus on what you don't want to think about; instead direct your thoughts to a better destination. This is what Paul meant when he wrote, "Set your mind on things above, not on things on the earth" (Colossians 3:2). I've found the best way to do this is through reciting Scripture and singing worship songs. Paul also pointed to the power of this strategy: "Let the word of Christ dwell in you richly in all wisdom, teaching and admonishing one another in psalms and hymns and spiritual songs, singing with grace in your hearts to the Lord" (v. 16). Scripture puts your mind and heart into an airplane mode that makes it impervious to low-living, low-thinking communication that we are so often bombarded by.

At the end of the book, I've included some of my favorite verses, which I encourage you to look through. Memorize your favorites. Whenever a thought doesn't pass inspection, use one of the verses to evict that thought.

By the way, I am halfway through a trip right now, and I just discovered in my backpack a five-inch pocket knife that I managed to get through security. And I have one more segment to go.

The funniest part is that when I went through security, my bag was pulled aside for additional screening. When the TSA agent looked through it, he pulled out a backup phone battery and told me that that was what had tripped the sensors. Neither of us knew about the knife, which was right below the battery.

So while writing this chapter on the importance of TSA screenings, I've been able to carry an *extremely sharp knife* onto an airplane. If the rest of this book is just blank pages, you'll know why. I'll be sitting in a federal prison somewhere, serving my time, because I didn't have TSA on the brain.

THE SECRET TO A
MISERABLE LIFE

*How much larger your life would be if
your self could become smaller in it.*

—G. K. CHESTERTON

I lay on my back in a hospital gown, an IV in my arm. I closed my eyes and couldn't bear to watch as a female nurse lifted the bottom edge of the gown, revealing all my God-given secrets. I was fourteen years old. It was humiliating. If I could have died on the spot I would have. The nurse was nice enough and professional about it, but this was a first for fourteen-year-old me.

It got worse. She and another nurse, this one a man who apologized for his cold hands, told me they had to shave me in preparation for surgery.

It had all started in middle school. Unbeknownst to me,

my vision had gotten bad. Teachers would ask me what was on the chalkboard, and I would tell them, "I don't know"—not to be smart but because I genuinely couldn't see it. It was just blurry. When they pressed me to read the sentence or the math problem and I still wouldn't comply, they interpreted my lack of response as defiance, and I ended up in trouble.

I can still feel myself in that sixth grade English and math class at Dwight D. Eisenhower, staring at a red-faced, irate teacher and a blurry chalkboard that I couldn't read. Eventually my mom caught me squinting, put two and two together, and realized I needed to have my vision checked. The optometrist was shocked I had made it as long as I had with such bad vision and immediately prescribed glasses. On the drive home I remember being able to see every leaf on every tree. Everything looked so bright and vivid. I was like, "Wow, so this is what the world looks like!"

You would think glasses would have solved my problems, but they just created new ones, because I really hated the way I looked in them. Ironically these round, tortoise-flecked frames are currently on the bestsellers shelf at Warby Parker, but back in the 1990s, they just seemed lame. Add to my dorky glasses the fact that I was asthmatic, one of the smallest in my grade, and had buck teeth. By eighth grade I was doing all I could to cope with the volcano of insecurity welling up within me.

There was a group of cool skater kids in my grade, and I wanted them to like me more than anything. They wore wide-leg JNCO jeans, Airwalk shoes, and T-shirts emblazoned with words like *Mossimo*, *No Fear*, *Rusty*, and *Billabong*. They listened to Nirvana and wore their backpacks with both straps. I wanted to fit in with them and to be in their circle.

I went to impressive lengths in order to be like these people. I saved up money to order a skateboard from a CCS catalog and bought clothes that I could see them wearing. Their shoes were all beat up from riding skateboards, but mine were brand new, and try as I might to kick flip and ollie to break them in, I decided to speed up the process by taking sandpaper to them to make me look legit. But all of these actions were just a mask. I was a poser.

I followed them around and hung out at the periphery. With time they sort of accepted my presence. But I always felt like a fake; I knew I wasn't one of them. This was most obvious because of the nickname they gave me: "Ratboy." I laughed it off, but it stung. I felt like their pet rather than their friend.

Sometimes I would say something they thought was funny, and they would all laugh—which to me felt like snorting a line of cocaine. No, it was better than drugs; I drank and smoked cigarettes and marijuana with them a few times, and those just made me feel empty and sick. This was much more addicting. It was pure, uncut, premium grade validation—and I was hooked.

Nothing about being around these people was good for me. One of the things they taught me was how to huff markers, paint, or Wite-Out to get high. They would also make each other faint to get a head rush. One of the guys would breathe as fast as possible for a minute, and then three or four of his friends would push on his chest as he held his breath until he passed out, crumpling to the ground. Sometimes they would combine the two by breathing the fumes of a toxic marker before trying to black themselves out. It boggles my mind that I was stupid enough to participate in either of these things. I could have been killed.

A couple of girls who were their groupies would rotate through the guys, hooking up with them at random. I befriended those girls, and they treated me like a little brother. How they were passed around really bothered me and broke my heart, but it also frustrated me to feel like I was perma-trapped in the friend zone with them and wasn't considered romantic material.

One of my least favorite things about being around this group was the hazing I faced as the outsider trying to become part of their world. Besides calling me "Ratboy," they also looked for any unsuspecting moment to swing a kick between my legs. It wasn't just me; they would do it to each other too. This was the era of Beavis and Butthead, and physical violence pretty much went along with friendship as a rite of passage. Multiple times a week one of them would rack me when my guard was down, and I would crumple to the ground like an empty can that had been crushed as they all laughed and high-fived at how funny it was. I remember one time coming to in the locker room after they had "fainted" me, and they were all busting up laughing. Confused, I looked around for explanation, and one of them told me that just as I passed out one of them had racked me with gusto.

I read not too long ago that for most Americans middle school is the worst time in their lives. It sure was no cake walk for me.

Eventually something went wrong in my nether regions. I'll spare you the details, but things got crazy inflamed. When it got worse instead of better, I begrudgingly told my parents I needed to go to the doctor. I played dumb as to what could possibly have caused the inflammation, unwilling to concede

I had been kicked in the groin one too many times by my "friends" at school. It shocked me when the doctor told me that the injury required surgery.

I never told any of the kids at school what had happened. I healed completely and made sure I didn't get close enough for any of them to take another kick. I moved on, but the experience scarred me—emotionally and otherwise. At the end of eighth grade, nearly all the comments in my yearbook from this crew were addressed to "Ratboy" and included touching statements like "Don't fall for the cheese" and "Watch out for the traps." Who needs enemies when you have friends?

The next year several of them moved away or transferred to different schools, and the group more or less broke up. I eventually made better friends who didn't bully me, my growth spurt finally kicked in, I convinced my parents to allow me to get contact lenses, and I developed a shell of humor and sarcasm to defend myself from appearing weak.

Looking back on the experience, I'm not angry at the kids who picked on me. I'm mostly sad at myself for wanting them to like me and for not respecting myself to the point that I put myself in harm's way.

MASKING OUR INSECURITIES

You don't have to be a psychologist to know that facing this kind of stress affects who you become. These difficult moments planted in me the seeds of insecurity that blossomed into a harvest of heartache.

Here is my confession: I care what other people think

about me way too much, and I really want to be noticed and accepted. I want other people to like me because I have trouble liking myself. I need others to validate me. So many of my life's problems have come from a longing to be in the "in circle" and have a seat at that table. To be liked, celebrated, approved. I forget that I *already* have those things in Jesus. With a Drew-Barrymore-in-*50-First-Dates*-like amnesia, I look for lesser versions of things that are already mine.

I've come to understand that wanting to please people is completely motivated by selfishness, because it ends up pointing back to me and how I feel about myself. I have also discovered that the more you think about yourself, the more wretched you feel. Narcissism leads to loneliness. Living out of your insecurities is the secret to a miserable life.

It's time to let the wolf rise and declare war on miserable living.

I doubt I am the only person who has ended up having surgery due to insecurity. Mine just happened to be to fix an injury done to me by people I wanted to like me; perhaps yours was to enhance your body or change your appearance so others would like you. Toe-may-toe, toe-mah-toe.

My theory is that none of us ever really leaves middle school. The stakes get higher, but the desire to please people never goes away. Instead of worrying that your friends will figure out your Airwalk shoes have been sanded, you might worry that your friends will discover your purse is just a Louis Vuitton knockoff. Instead of chasing likes from a circle of kids at school, you're chasing likes on Instagram. Instead of comparing the size of your ollies to those of your buddies, you're comparing the size of your paycheck and the square footage of your house.

Insecurity is a lack of confidence. It comes from uncertainty about your worth, value, or place in the world. Insecurity is believing that you aren't enough—pretty enough, rich enough, strong enough, smart enough—and that you don't have what it takes, that you aren't one of the cool kids, that the lies and harsh words people have spoken over your life are true. That you are damaged goods, and if people really knew you, they wouldn't accept you. It is feeling out of your league, inadequate, and unqualified.

Do you struggle with any of that? Me too.

As a result, we hide behind defense mechanisms that, like masks, cover our true selves.

- One such mechanism is *lashing out*—trying to make other people feel small because you feel small and misery loves company. You wear an "I'm better than you" mask that you rarely remove. The fallacy of this defense is that you can never rise by cutting other people down to size. It doesn't achieve what you intend.
- There's the *"I'm fine" defense*—pretending that everything is okay and acting as though you don't care what anyone thinks. This is the "sticks and stones can break my bones but words can never hurt me" response, but it is only a veneer covering up sadness within. You wear a smiley-face mask that projects everything is cool, even though you're crying underneath.
- *Ramping up your sex appeal* is another coping strategy. Cleavage-revealing tops, shorter skirts, post after post of your body in skimpy bathing suits, or nonstop bicep-building and pec-pumping pics at the gym so you can

have a Zac Efron *Baywatch* body by summer. This is the *Fifty Shades of Grey* mask; you crave attention, seeking validation of your attractiveness, hoping for the approval that comes from being noticed.

- My main defense mechanism is *the **funny-guy veneer.*** I need people to laugh, to think I am amusing. I wore the mask of class clown because I was picked on. The tough shell grew to protect me from feeling weak and from feeling as though I didn't matter. You, too, might have this tendency if you turn everything into a joke or make self-deprecating remarks. Humor serves as a deflection to divert the attention away from what you feel insecure about.

- Then there's *the **religious defense***—the "I'm so holy" mask. People who hide behind their religion brag about how many Bible verses they've memorized, or how frequently they go to church, or how much they give to the poor, or what they've done for God. Jesus responded to this defense mechanism directly when he warned his disciples not to be like the religious-mask-wearing Pharisees:

> Watch yourselves carefully so you don't get contaminated with Pharisee yeast, Pharisee phoniness. You can't keep your true self hidden forever; before long you'll be exposed. You can't hide behind a religious mask forever; sooner or later the mask will slip and your true face will be known. You can't whisper one thing in private and preach the opposite in public; the day's coming when those whispers will be repeated all over town. (Luke 12:1–3 THE MESSAGE)

The problem with the religious mask is that, as *The Message* author Eugene Peterson observed, "The primary concern of the spiritual life isn't what we do for God but what God does for us." We mistakenly think his blessings are determined by our behavior, but the truth is that his blessings come first, completely undeserved, and that is what helps us change our behavior. It's called grace. And it. changes. everything.

- Earlier I wrote of my experience with *trying to be like everyone else*—the "Clone Wars" mask. Let me remind you that this mask never goes away; it just becomes more expensive to keep up with the Joneses. For instance, how much of our credit card debt comes from trying to stay on track with those in our peer groups?

- Sometimes we respond to insecurity by *numbing ourselves*. Consuming drugs and alcohol, viewing pornography, or overloading on social media or shopping are like putting a zombie mask over our emotions. Why feel sad when you can have an instant hit of dopamine from Amazon Prime? The problem with numbing is that, to quote Brené Brown, "We cannot selectively numb emotions. When we numb the painful emotions, we also numb the positive emotions." Eventually you end up without pain or pleasure, joy or sadness. You just feel nothing.

- And of course there is *compensation*—the classic response to insecurity famously demonstrated by Napoleon, who made up for his height with exaggerated bravado. Compensation looks like constantly name-dropping, one-upping, and bragging about your accomplishments; turning everything into a competition. This gold-plated, diamond-crusted mask is not only draining to those around you who constantly feel like they are watching a show, but it is exhausting to keep up pretenses. The only thing more taxing than being around an insecure person is being an insecure person.

When you live in a place of insecurity, it's impossible to enjoy the journey, because you're always afraid of letting your mask slip. It's ironic that we put on masks in hopes of finding love and acceptance, but people can't love someone they don't know. What they're falling in love with isn't you; it's your mask, a superficial version of you, a costume you've carefully curated.

Think long and hard about the long-term consequences of worming your way into relationships by not being authentically you. What you wear to obtain, you must wear to retain.

Mask On. Mask Off

The payoff for wearing a mask is being stuck in it. If you get the job with the mask, you have to wear the mask every day at work. If you get the relationship with the mask, you have to wear the mask whenever you're with that person. "Fake it till you make it" is sometimes good advice (in the third section of the book, I'll talk about how it can be powerful when it comes to doing the right thing when you don't feel like doing it), but when it comes to being fake as a way of covering over your insecurities, you never actually make it. If you fake it, you'll have to keep faking it.

Author Donald Miller wrote in his book *Scary Close* (an

incredible, in-depth look at what we are talking about in this chapter) that "honesty is the soil that intimacy grows in." Rich relationships prosper only when you are real and transparent. Deception erodes the beautiful "naked and unashamed" kind of vulnerability that is the bedrock of healthy, fulfilling relationships.

Which defense mechanisms do you struggle with? You might need a whole closet for your masks, as each is suited for a particular situation. That's when it gets tricky. When you have different responses for different situations, it's hard to remember which mask is for which day. As the Walter Scott poem goes, "Oh! what a tangled web we weave / when first we practise to deceive!" It's so much less work to just be yourself.

What caused you to put the mask on in the first place? Why do you resort to latex over your skin? I think it's because you and I don't feel like we're enough. We believe the lies—the lies that say you are how much you make or what you've achieved: *I am my GPA. I am my waist size. I am my followers on social media. I am only as successful as last Sunday's attendance at church or the rating of my podcast.*

To paraphrase another concept from *Scary Close* that resonates with my experience: it wasn't always this way. When we were kids, we could just play. We jumped off swings and built things with rocks and smiled at the sun. But at some point along the way, we faced significant hurt or embarrassment for the first time. At some point along the way, we realized that we weren't quite like the other kids, or we didn't live up to our parents' exacting standards. And because we felt inadequate, like we weren't enough, we developed a phony exterior to show people. Craving love and acceptance, we put masks on because we didn't feel like we were worthy of love without them.

The biggest problem with defense mechanisms is this: when you put a mask on, you are masking yourself off from God's blessing.

You know how when you paint a room, you first have to tape around the edges of what you don't want the paint to get on—the light switch, the ceiling, the floorboards? The paint only goes where the tape is not. That's why it's hard for God's blessing to reach what you've covered over. God constantly seeks to shower you with grace. He wants to cover you with favor, to coach you with his love, to give you his best and his blessings. He wants your cup to run over. He wants to anoint your head with oil. He has been dreaming about it from before the foundation of the earth. But he can't use who you wish you were—only who you really are. Your mask is holding you back.

Don't miss this! You are fearfully and wonderfully made (Psalm 139:14). You are unique; you are beautiful, a work of art. You are God's poem, his masterpiece. You are what he thinks, not what you think.

When you are filled with wonder and not pretense, as you were as a child, you are as God intended you to be. Anything you do that's phony or a lie—any of these affectations that are not true to how God built you—is masking tape.

The cure for insecurity is understanding your true identity. When the Old Testament judge Gideon doubted himself and tried to put on a mask, God told him he was a mighty man of valor so he would know his true identity, trust in God, and accomplish great things (Judges 6:12). For this reason, God refused to let Gideon fight the Midianites with the thirty-two

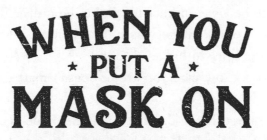

WHEN YOU
★ PUT A ★
MASK ON

YOU ARE
MASKING
YOURSELF
OFF

FROM GOD'S
BLESSING

thousand soldiers he marshalled, insisting instead that he fight with a meager three hundred by his side as he faced off against an army of one hundred thousand plus. The soldiers he had amassed had become another mask, but God dismantled it to get him out from what he was hiding behind. (Promise me you'll read the story in Judges 6 soon.)

When you know who you are, it doesn't matter what you are not.

You are loved by God. That's why he made you, why he saved you. Why he shed the blood of his Son and filled you with his Spirit. Why he gave you a calling. You're loved by God! You don't need approval from anyone else, because the only likes that really matter come from heaven—and they are already yours.

God didn't get stuck with you; he *chose* you. You weren't a white elephant gift; God picked you knowing your faults and the skeletons in your closet. He's never been disgusted or surprised or shocked by anything you've done.

Whenever you find yourself thinking, *I don't. I can't. I'm not*, respond right back: *I do. I am. I have. I can—because I'm loved by God!*

You are not your career; you are not your collection of shoes or followers; you are not your car or your job or the table you sit at in the school cafeteria. Instead, put your value in being God's daughter or son, in being loved by him.

The good news for us insecure, mask-wearing phonies is that we can choose to take the mask off. That's scary, I know. You might have been wearing one so long you don't know what life would look like without it, but let me tell you: it looks like freedom.

GOD
DIDN'T GET
STUCK
— WITH —
YOU
HE
CHOSE
YOU

As writer Ralph Waldo Emerson put it, "God will not have his work made manifest by cowards." It takes bravery to be vulnerable. You'll feel terrified. You'll want to put the mask back on and hide once more. But the only way to get to victory is by going through vulnerability. Only by embracing who you are can you become who you were born to be.

If I could talk to eighth-grade Levi, I wouldn't lecture him about how terrible his buddies are and how they are going to kick him in the crotch until he needs surgery. I *would* reassure him that, at age thirty-six, everything would still be in working order, and that he and his beautiful wife would eventually have five kids. I would hope to help younger Levi see that, instead of showing up *empty* and looking to receive affirmation from kids at school, by looking to Jesus his tank would be constantly *full*. Instead of needing to receive value from the wrong sources, he could impart value and give grace—even to those who are harsh, because who knows what difficult battles they are fighting that made them feel the need to be cruel.

And I would tell him that God can do huge things with little people. With God's help, a ratboy can change the world.

2 ♦

DECLARE
WAR ON

WHAT YOU SAY
WHAT YOU SAY DETERMINES WHAT YOU SEE

2 ♦

MIND YOUR WORDS

*You can easily judge the character of a man by
how he treats those who can do nothing for him.*

—FORBES, 1972

I've been a hospital patient in England—twice, separated by ten years, for the same accident. No joke. My life's weird.

I was even in the same emergency room. (The English don't call it the *ER*, by the way; they call it *A&E*, which is confusing, because to us Americans A&E is a TV channel nobody watches. But in England *A&E* stands for "Accidents and Emergency.")

There are a lot of things lost in translation between England and the United States. I'm sure it's annoying to them to hear what we have done to the Queen's English, but I have just as difficult a time understanding their words as they do understanding ours.

Imagine you're visiting England and get a craving for the Doritos your English friend is eating. If you say, "Hey, give me some of those chips," she'd be like, "Oh, you mean these crisps?" When the English talk about *chips*, they're referring to French fries.

You go to your apartment; they go to their *flat*. Your elevator is their *lift*. A shopping cart at the grocery store is a *push trolley*. You throw the garbage not in the trash can, but in the *bin*, and the trash bag is the *bin liner*. A diaper is a *nappy*, and a stroller is a *pram*.

This is not normal, people.

There is one English word I do prefer: instead of saying *watch out*, they use the word *mind*. For instance, when you get on the subway (or *the tube*, as they call it) in London, both a sign and a recorded voice warn you about the crevice between the train platform and the train: "Mind the gap."

Similarly, if there's a low overhang that you might bang your head on (many buildings there were built hundreds of years ago, and people were apparently shorter back then), you'll see a sign that says, "Mind your head"—meaning, be mindful that you don't hit your head.

The more I think about it, the more this phrasing makes sense. You can't very well *watch* your head (unless you have a mirror) because your eyes are mounted on it. But you *can* be mindful of it. And if you don't, you'll do what I did. Twice.

In 2001 in Yorkshire, I smashed my head into a low overhang that I didn't see and lacerated my scalp. I was in my flat, and when I heard the phone ring, I jumped—right into the low doorway above me. Sheets of blood ran down my face. I waited in the hospital lobby (where they didn't even have A&E to watch on TV) for several hours, until they could superglue my head shut.

If you have read my first book, *Through the Eyes of a Lion,* you will remember the next story. Thirteen years later, I was back in England, and once again, I didn't mind my head. This time, I cut my head open—in the same spot—while leaning under a low window. And I found myself in the same hospital, where they glued my head shut. Again.

All that to say, the words *mind your head* have become very near and dear to me. In this section, as we lay down the second card, I am going to tell you about another important thing for you to be mindful of: the things you say. This includes the words you speak to others, the words you speak to yourself, the words you speak about your life, and the words you speak when you are afraid.

Words are powerful. You can't win the war with the version of yourself you don't want to be if you focus only on sticks and stones and think that words can never hurt you. Here are some of the big ideas we'll explore in this card:

- You can alter how you feel through changing the way you speak.
- You don't have to say everything you feel like saying.
- The words you speak over people can change the courses of their lives.
- The person you talk to more than anyone else is yourself.

My Big. Fat. Stupid Mouth

My cheeks flush. My jaw clenches. I can feel my stomach tighten, and suddenly I'm aware of how hot the back of my neck is. I'm angry. I feel disrespected and powerless, like I'm being treated unfairly or attacked without provocation. I experience the all-too-familiar sensation of falling. Then, as fast as thunder follows lightning, a volley of words forms in my chest, a combination of battery acid and alphabet soup. In a flash I think of three hundred things to say that will cut the person in front of me down to size.

I have faced that feeling in airports, restaurants, department stores, hotels, cars, planes, grocery stores, the office, and my own home. I have felt it while hunched over my laptop or squinting at my phone.

I want to spit venom, breathe fire, and lash out. It seems like the situation would improve if I could land the perfect string of vitriolic sentences on my target. Curse words are rare but not absent from my arsenal. Usually the words that come to mind are passive aggressive, cutting, and dripping with sarcasm. I am almost always stunned by the meanness I am capable of, and it catches me off guard to see how quickly I become a small, indignant child ready to hurl rocks because I have gotten hurt. In those moments my goal is to dispatch as many of my enemies as I can with as few words as possible, inflicting maximum devastation per syllable.

My tendency toward verbal beatdowns has its origins in those traumatic middle school days, when the cruelty of the words like "Ratboy" washed over me. The name-calling should have made me never want to be mean to others, but instead, I used it as an excuse to develop a sharp tongue. I resort to blistering comebacks anytime I feel cornered. On my worst days, I lash out at those closest to me. My parents, siblings, wife, kids, and coworkers have all been on the receiving end of my seemingly untamable tongue.

I hate the two or three seconds of silence just after I let loose a comment that I should have contained. I see the words floating through the air like a missile, and I realize a moment too late how much they are going to sting. But just as I reach to pull them back from the sky, they strike true, and bitter remorse churns in my heart when I see the sadness and betrayal in the eyes of someone who trusts me.

My wife once asked me why I don't enjoy Scrabble, and I told her it's because it feels like work. I couldn't bring myself to play Words with Friends either. Me and words are plenty good enough friends—perhaps a little too good.

Words are my life. They are what I do. I have spent thousands and thousands of hours laboring over very precise wording and arranging outlines, message points, chapters, paragraphs, sentences. I mull over plays on words, end rhymes, beginning rhymes, alliteration. As a child, I would obsess over whether the sentences I said or heard had an even or odd number of syllables. My mom would (and, if I am completely honest, sometimes Jennie still does) catch me silently mouthing something I just said a second time to roll it around and test its rhythmic quality.

For every sermon I write there might be three or four different versions that don't get preached. When I finish this chapter, I'm going to go finalize a message that has been *killing* me because I couldn't find the right title. The sermon is about living beyond "bucket lists"—you know, those things you want to do before you die, like swim with sharks and camp in the Grand Canyon. Last night at dinner, after several hours of agonizing how to articulate that idea in as few words as possible, I had an epiphany when my daughter Clover said the word *bucket* in a completely unrelated context. I shouted, "KICKING THE BUCKET LIST!" as though I had just discovered gravity—because it completely conveys what I want to communicate and juxtaposes two familiar ideas in an unexpected way.

Here's the problem: an unguarded strength is a double weakness. If you flip over any virtue, you'll find vice on the bottom.

Whatever comes naturally to you can easily become a problem for you. Ask Solomon, the wisest person who ever lived, who made some of the most foolish decisions anyone has ever made.

There's no other area that is easier (for me) to mess up with, and that has caused more heartache afterward, than talking. I've shot my mouth off and felt remorse so regularly that it is a great source of sadness for me. I measure how well a meeting went not by the number of good ideas I had or whether the content was covered but by whether it ends without me having said something I want to take back.

You know that feeling when you walk away from a conversation and the perfect insult comes to your mind just a minute too late? ("Well, the Jerk Store called, and they're running out of you!") The French have a term for it: *esprit de escalier,* or the witty comeback you think of after you've left the situation. There is science behind why that happens: when you're in a confrontation, the limbic portion of your brain kicks into fight-or-flight mode, allocating all available resources into keeping you alive; unfortunately, both cleverness and people skills suffer. Once the moment passes, the blood that was being diverted to your muscles and to your vision with a shot of adrenaline returns to the rational part of your brain, so you are able to think of what you couldn't in the moment. I wish I had that feeling more often. The feeling I have more regularly is, *why didn't I put a hand over my mouth and not say the thing I thought of?* Tragically, words are like toothpaste; once they're out of the tube, there's no putting them back in.

The Power of the Tongue

The book of Proverbs says that the tongue contains the power of both life and death (Proverbs 18:21). It's like a tiny nuclear reactor capable of being both an energy plant that lights up a town and a bomb that can destroy a city.

I read that Orville Wright was heartsick over the use of airplanes in World War II because they allowed mankind the option of raining bombs from the sky. It disturbed him to know that he had created something that would do so much harm, yet he didn't regret the invention. What reassured him was knowing that all things that can do much good can also do great evil.

Bricks can be used to build hospitals or be thrown through windows. Water can quench a thirst or flood a city. Likewise, words are neutral in and of themselves; it's how you use them that determines whether they are good or bad.

That is the argument James makes in one of the most powerful statements on speech ever put into words (pun intended):

> Indeed, we put bits in horses' mouths that they may obey us, and we turn their whole body. Look also at ships: although they are so large and are driven by fierce winds, they are turned by a very small rudder wherever the pilot desires.

BRICKS
CAN BE
USED TO
BUILD
HOSPITALS
OR BE
THROWN
THROUGH
WINDOWS

Even so the tongue is a little member and boasts great things. See how great a forest a little fire kindles! And the tongue is a fire, a world of iniquity. The tongue is so set among our members that it defiles the whole body, and sets on fire the course of nature; and it is set on fire by hell. For every kind of beast and bird, of reptile and creature of the sea, is tamed and has been tamed by mankind. But no man can tame the tongue. It is an unruly evil, full of deadly poison. With it we bless our God and Father, and with it we curse men, who have been made in the similitude of God. Out of the same mouth proceed blessing and cursing. My brethren, these things ought not to be so. (James 3:3–10)

James explained that one tiny spark—a cigarette thrown out a car window or an improperly doused campfire—can lead to an inferno that burns down a whole forest. In the same way, a single sentence can alter your life: "I love you." "Will you marry me?" "It's a boy." "I want a divorce." "I forgive you." "I'm sorry."

A sentence can devastate: "We're going to have to let you go." "It's cancer." "There's nothing more we can do."

But it can just as easily cause you to celebrate: "You're being promoted!" "You have the golden ticket!" "Your long-lost aunt left you an enormous inheritance!"

Words can cost you your job; Don Imus had a successful radio career but he was brought down by uttering a racial slur. Words can cost you your life; mouth off to the wrong person and get yourself killed.

When I read what James wrote about the tongue's deadly poison, I can't help but think of the komodo dragon, the largest living lizard. Komodo dragons are stocky and built low to the ground. Even though they're not fast, they can kill pigs and even cows with their venom. Careless words, too, can cause hurt—sometimes even kill.

Besides poison and fire, which have obvious dangers, James used the analogies of horseback riding and boating—two fun activities that can quickly go wrong.

You might remember that the actor Christopher Reeve, who played Superman in the original films (long before the Man of Steel got in a fight with Batman and joined the Justice League), broke his neck jumping over a fence on his horse and became a quadrapalegic who needed a wheelchair for the rest of his life. Boating accidents can also cause great harm. I remember a horrific accident that happened where I live in Montana. A ski boat had stopped to pick up a fallen water-skier. While the boat was idling, a passenger jumped off the boat to go to the bathroom—only the driver of the boat didn't know. When he looked back and saw the skier was far behind him, he put the boat in reverse and drove over the guy peeing in the water. The driver wasn't even aware the other man was there, right behind the boat. Rescuers were able to save the injured man's life, but he still lost his foot in the accident.

Just as heredity controls what kind of tongue you have—whether you can roll it up or how long it is—heredity is also the reason our tongues are so destructive. We read in Romans 5:12 that it's our sin nature that makes our words so dangerous: "Through one man sin entered the world, and death through sin, and thus death spread to all men, because all sinned." Fortunately, whatever can be used for evil can be reclaimed and used for good.

The tongue can be set on fire by hell, but it can also be set on fire by heaven. While under control of the Holy Spirit, Peter—who had cursed Christ and denied knowing him—preached the gospel to the saving of two thousand souls on the day of Pentecost. Proverbs 25:11 tells us, "A word fitly spoken is like apples of gold in settings of silver." If your speech is filled with grace (Colossians 4:6), your words will have the same impact salt (or Tabasco sauce) does on food—they will make things better! Then your words can build people up, share the gospel, pray for the sick. Your words can encourage, comfort, reassure, and make people laugh. Proverbs 27:17 says, "As iron sharpens iron, so a friend sharpens a friend" (NLT). Sometimes you need to speak difficult words that are necessary to help people become who they were born to be. In a sense, love will ask you to stab your friends in the front. And that's a good thing!

When the tongue is working properly, it is both a spring that refreshes and a fruit tree that nourishes. A runaway horse is dangerous, and a boating accident can end in disaster; but when the bit is firmly in place, and the rudder steers correctly, you can enjoy scenery that is both beautiful and pleasurable.

Paul instructed the Ephesians to choose their words carefully: "Let no corrupt word proceed out of your mouth, but what is good for necessary edification, that it may impart grace to the hearers" (Ephesians 4:29). My high school youth pastor made me memorize that verse when I confided in him that I regularly got into trouble because of things I said. He advised me to process what I wanted to say through an Ephesians 4:29 filter before I spoke.

Consider *The Message*'s translation of this verse: "Watch the way you talk. Let nothing foul or dirty come out of your mouth. Say only what helps, each word a gift." What could

WHEN THE
TONGUE
IS WORKING
PROPERLY
IT IS BOTH A
SPRING
★ THAT ★
REFRESHES
★ AND A ★
FRUIT
TREE THAT
NOURISHES

happen if the words you used weren't foul or dirty but rather were gifts for those you were speaking to?

I still fight daily to keep my tongue in check. If I let my guard down, it's so easy for me to relapse. I may have banged my head into the wall in England only twice, but I've made a bloody mess many, many more times by not minding my words. But as the wolf has risen in my heart to fight this battle, I've seen enormous benefits. Throughout the next three chapters, I'm going to challenge you to wage war on the words that you speak. If Jesus is the Lord of your life, he must be the Lord of your lips too.

Famous Last Words

Have you ever thought about what your last words might be?

American patriot Nathan Hale's last words were "I only regret that I have but one life to lose for my country," which mimicked a line from a popular play called *Cato*. Then there's William Owen "Buckey" O'Neill, one of the members of Teddy Roosevelt's Rough Riders during the Spanish-American War. Buckey was smoking a cigarette and joking with his troops while under fire when he was warned by a sergeant of the danger he was in. His last words were: "Sergeant, the Spanish bullet ain't made that will kill me!" Guess how he died? By a Spanish bullet. Then there's the great evangelist D. L. Moody, who said on his deathbed, "I see earth receding and heaven is opening. God is calling me." According to Steve Jobs's sister Mona, the Apple founder's last words were, "Oh wow. Oh wow. Oh wow."

There are no more powerful last words than what we find in the pages of the Bible. Joshua told the children of Israel, "Behold, this day I am going the way of all the earth. And you know in all your hearts and in all your souls that not one thing has failed of all the good things which the Lord your God spoke concerning you. All have come to pass for you; not one word of them has failed" (Joshua 23:14). What authority Joshua could speak with! He leveraged his experiences to build up the faith of the people he loved and had led.

The most stunning last words in Scripture come from a man who used them to give his life to Jesus. With his dying breath, the thief on the cross turned to Jesus and said, "Lord, remember me when You come into Your kingdom" (Luke 23:42). And though he had lived a life of crime and sin, the man was saved. Jesus said, "Assuredly, I say to you, today you will be with Me in Paradise." (v. 43). Doesn't that tell you something about the love of God? There is no one so far gone that they can't be saved. No matter what.

Speaking of Jesus, his last words are unrivaled in their significance. First he said, "*Tetelestai*," which means "It is finished," or paid in full (John 19:30). He had suffered for all the sin of the world, which had been laid on him. And then, having finished the mission given to him by God, he said, "Father, into Your hands I commit My spirit" (Luke 23:46), which comes from Psalm 31:5. In Jesus' day, that psalm was a common bedtime prayer. Mary might have recited it to Jesus every night before he went to sleep. Perhaps she even whispered it to him as he slept in the manger the night he was born. It's possible that she recited these words to him thousands and thousands of times as he grew.

She could never have known she was teaching him to die!

But Jesus wasn't just praying these words out of nostalgia for his childhood. He left us footprints to follow when it comes time for us to die. Stephen, the first follower of Jesus to be killed for his faith after Jesus' resurrection, recognized what Jesus had modeled: "They stoned Stephen as he was calling on God and saying, 'Lord Jesus, receive my spirit.' Then he knelt down and cried out with a loud voice, 'Lord, do not charge them with this sin.' And when he had said this, he fell asleep" (Acts 7:59–60).

Here is the power of such a prayer: you don't have to fear dying if you know where you're going. If you have given your life to Jesus, then death isn't *leaving* home; it's *going* home. Here's the fine print: only *you* can commit your spirit to God.

It takes the cooperation of 72 different muscles to produce speech. On average 16,000 words come out of your mouth per day. That adds up to a whopping 860.3 million in a lifetime. Out of all the nouns, verbs, adjectives, and articles that could ever come from your mouth, the most important, by far, are words you choose to speak trusting your soul to God's hands. I recommend you don't wait until your deathbed to say them. Why not right now? You're not too messed up; you're not a hopeless case. God promised that "*whoever* calls on the name of the LORD shall be saved" (Romans 10:13, emphasis mine). Before you turn the page to read the next chapter, you could turn something brand new over in your soul, beginning a new season as a child of God. Only when you are ready to face death are you truly ready to face life. Yes, it's important to mind your head, but it's even more vital to mind your soul.

IF YOU SAY SO

God's main business is blessing, not cursing.

—Eugene Peterson

My family is a Disneyland family. We love the place. There is truly a magic and a charm about it (and, yes, a price tag to match). Pass through the gates and enter a land of tomorrow, fantasy, adventure, whatever you feel like. I love how much attention Disney pays to the smallest details. They work so hard to ensure that even the lines you wait in are part of the little world you're exploring. (Also, it reassures me to know that Mickey used to be named Mortimer and that he was originally a rat. That tells you that small tweaks, not huge shifts, will lead you to enormous breakthroughs. The tiny difference between Mickey and Mortimer seems slight but has billion-dollar implications.)

Walt Disney's intention was for visitors to experience

something special, that imagination and story would swirl around them as they explored the parks, rode the rides, and spent the day in his kingdom of magic.

It's hard not to feel your heart beat a little faster as you walk through the gates and catch a glimpse of the giant Mickey Mouse built out of flowers on the hill just past the ticket agents. You forget your cares as you get swept up in something creative and all-encompassing.

I went to a Disney park only once as a child, and it was pretty much the high mark of my upbringing. When my wife and I moved to California, we bought season passes and went regularly, even if it was just for an hour to walk around, people watch, and have dessert. Taking my kids to the park has been exponentially more full of joy than I could have predicted.

My favorite thing about Disney parks is the smell. Disney goes to extraordinary lengths to control your experience, and they know that memory and emotion are inextricably connected to scent. This is because the olfactory nerve, which carries information about smells to the brain, runs right by the amygdala, the part of the brain that stores memory and emotional information.

When you ride Soarin' Around the World in California Adventure, you can smell the ocean while you fly over the sea. You can catch the scent of dirt kicked up by a stampede you fly over while riding on the back of a banshee on Flight of Passage, an *Avatar*-inspired ride in Animal Kingdom that almost made me cry. When Heimlich's Chew Chew Train takes you through a watermelon, you can smell that too. The way the rides and the food vendors pump scent in the air makes the experience take on a different dimension. You can smell your way through the park, from the entrance to the exit.

The combination of certain sounds and smells around Disneyland in Orange County has the effect on me that eating ratatouille had on those in the Pixar movie by the same name: it transports me back in time. I find myself zooming through the pages of my life. I am a little boy, a newly married husband. I'm walking hand-in-hand with a little girl who is now in heaven. I'm carrying each of my daughters on my shoulders on their first daddy-daughter trip to the park, the castle in our sights. These memories flood my brain while I push my son, Lennox, in a stroller on *his* first trip to the park.

It's hard not to get caught up and carried away when you sense so much in the air. None of it is by mistake. Every inch of the magic you experience at Disneyland is carefully, intentionally, and painstakingly designed by Imagineers. The atmosphere is charged with excitement, because Imagineers built it that way. They envisioned a concept in their minds, then put it down on paper; eventually the materials were printed, fabricated, cut, and sown, and the finished product has been lovingly and diligently maintained.

This is the same kind of passion and dedication you need to successfully fight the battle that wages within you for control of your life. God intends for you to be surrounded by an atmosphere of faith, but you have to intentionally create that atmosphere. And more than anything else, that requires your words.

Naming Rights

Let's back up. In the last chapter, I cautioned you about choosing your words carefully and warned you about the danger of destroying others with what you say. In this chapter, I'd like to give you the practical tools you'll need to use your words for good.

The first job God gave humans was to speak a word over something he made: "Now the LORD God had formed out of the ground all the wild animals and all the birds in the sky. He brought them to the man to see what he would name them; and whatever the man called each living creature, that was its name" (Genesis 2:19–20 NIV).

Did you catch that? Whatever man called the animal, that was its name. Adam's job was to speak, and what he spoke stuck. You have the same job. God brings to you a day, and your job is to give it a name—to declare something over it. Whatever you call it will stick.

Consider the implications:

When you wake up, you push through the usual morning disorientation: *My ponytail is still in. I should have taken that out before bed. I think my arm is asleep. How did that get positioned under me like that? What day is it? Tuesday. I should get up. But it's so warm in bed. If I don't get up now, I'll sleep another hour and be rushed all day.*

Stepping over laundry that is overflowing from the hamper, you trudge to the bathroom, keeping your eyes narrowed as you flip on the lights. You turn on the faucet and splash cold water on your face. It trickles over your fingers and down your cheeks like a thousand tiny rivers waking you up. Then comes the moment of truth, as for the first time today you pull your hands away and look at yourself in the mirror.

What do you see looking back at you? What do you choose to say in response to the person you see in the glass?

I am beautiful or *I am ugly?*

I am valuable or *I am not worthy of love?*

I am going to have a tremendous day or *I am so behind already.*

Whatever you say over what you see, that is what it is called.

Maybe, like me, you have gotten so good at listening to yourself that you have forgotten to speak to yourself. It's easy to drift along with the speakers of your soul blasting the play-by-play commentary of your naturally negative self. It's time you fire yourself as your personal critic and rehire yourself as a coach. You can alter how you feel through changing the way you speak.

This is war.

I woke up this morning to a worship song Alexa played for me on my Amazon Echo. I ate oatmeal and drank black coffee while I read my Bible and prayed. I haven't been on Instagram yet or purchased anything on Amazon. (If I reward my brain with dopamine before accomplishing anything, I'll be chasing that high all day; e-mail and social media are a treat I allow myself only when I have done something worthy of the reward.) Now I'm listening to very carefully selected music, and I'm burning a candle I use only when I'm writing. I'm wearing a pair of nonprescription "writing glasses," and when I put them on I am a writer who is not a coward or a procrastinator.

When I first woke up and thought about my writing, the usual intimidation began to tug at the edge of my mind: *You can't write. You'll get distracted. You tried to write on Monday but didn't get a single word out. No one—*

I muted that voice by speaking up: *This book is going to change lives. Writing it is going to help me and my readers. I*

★

YOU CAN
ALTER
HOW YOU
FEEL
— THROUGH —
CHANGING
THE
WAY YOU
SPEAK

★

can't wait to get started after I have my devotions. God has spoken to me, and he is going to speak through me!

I forced these words to come out of my mouth (quietly, because it was 6:13 a.m. and my kids were asleep), but I needed to hear myself speak positivity over the day in front of me:

My day job begins in a few hours. Before then I need to not only get some writing done but work out so I can be healthy and have energy. I speak in Seattle tonight, and Jennie's birthday is tomorrow, so I don't have even a spare five minutes to sit around in fear, anxiety, and self-pity. Ain't nobody got time for that.

And with that I showed up and got to work. And you can too.

The specific things I did might not help you win your war. Perhaps you hate oatmeal and candles give you a headache. That's okay. Figure out what works for you. You don't need to wear my "author glasses" to become the version of yourself you long to be; maybe there is a special ring you put on that helps you become a kind mom, or a special mug you drink your matcha out of that only brave, vulnerable, and self-aware people are allowed to touch. Winning the war within isn't one size-fits-all; it's a custom job for a tailor-made, one-of-a-kind masterpiece, because that's who you are and what your life is. You need to figure out what it takes for you to suit up so you can be your best when you show up.

How you speak determines how you feel. Stop listening to your fear, and put some faith in the air. The same way Disney Imagineers designed the atmosphere of the Cars Land exhibit to make you feel like you are on Route 66 in Radiator Springs, use your words to surround yourself with belief and strength.

Let It Be

You can't overemphasize the importance Scripture places on words. At creation God spoke the world into being (Genesis 1). At the incarnation God spoke himself into the world, and the Word became flesh in the person of Jesus, the living Word. (John 1:14). That should tell you something about the weight of words. At both the very beginning and then at the most critical, decisive moment in history, God's solution was to speak.

It should humble you to know that God has given you the same power of speech. That is part of the terrible privilege of being made in his image. Your speech can create, tear down, build, heal, or hurt.

When God hears you speak about your meeting as terrible, your car as crappy, your kids as ungrateful, your husband as lazy, your town as small, your house as cramped, his response is: *If you say so.* Because of the power he put into your tongue when he made you, he will allow the labels you speak into existence to stick. Consequently, you will have a terrible experience in your meeting, an unenjoyable ride in your crappy car. And you will find in your husband and kids a thousand examples of laziness and ingratitude. Your house will indeed shrink around you, as will the suddenly claustrophobic town you are trapped in. You will feel how you speak and find what you seek.

On the other hand, you can choose to talk about the meeting as one that will be challenging but important, full of opportunities to solve problems. You can choose to talk about how you are grateful to have a car, and how you are happy that your husband works hard to provide for your family, and how your children are going to learn gratitude from your example. That reminds you that you are thankful you don't live in that tiny studio apartment anymore, and while your current town may not be Los Angeles, it's charming in its own way. That prompts you to pray for a neighbor who's been on your mind, and when you're done, you text her a few words of encouragement. God's response to this new way of speaking is the same: *If you say so.*

Your words can unlock a life you love or one you loathe. It is up to you whether the self-fulfilling prophecies you articulate become a delight or a dungeon. Fortunately, as C. S. Lewis wrote, "The doors of hell are locked on the *inside.*" If you talked your way into your current mess, you can very likely talk your way out.

One of my favorite Bible stories illustrates the capacity your words have to set the tone for your faith and for your future. A centurion—an officer in the Roman army in charge of a hundred men—came to Jesus for help because his servant was seriously ill. Centurions were career soldiers, hardened men of war, easily identified by the red plumes they wore in their helmets. It was difficult to become a centurion, but once you got the position, you had it made. He had money, power, respect—in other words, he was living the dream.

On the other hand, slaves in the Roman empire had no rights; they weren't classified as human beings but rather as "living tools." Slaves significantly outnumbered the empire's 70 million citizens, and so maintaining the illusion of control was imperative for the masters, who knew there would be little they could do to stop a mutiny if the ants ever figured out that they didn't need to give all their food to the grasshoppers.

(Sorry not sorry. I told you I love Disney.) When a slave was sick and unable to work, masters were under no obligation to seek out medical attention, because they could just as easily buy a replacement.

You can see immediately that there was something different about this soldier. He showed no trace of cruelty, only tenderness as he sought help on behalf of his servant. The words he used show that he considers the young man to be like a son to him: "Lord, my servant is lying at home paralyzed, dreadfully tormented" (Matthew 8:6). In reference to Jesus, he used the word *Lord*; in Greek, the word is *kurios*, which means "king." This was nothing short of a profession of faith in Jesus as his sovereign.

In response to the centurion's pleas, Jesus immediately agreed to come to the man's home to treat his servant. But the centurion protested that there was no need for Jesus to enter his home. It would have been inconvenient for Jesus to travel, for one; second, if Jesus had entered the house of a Gentile, he would have been ceremonially defiled, and he would have had to go through a cleansing ritual before his daily life could continue. (Translation: he would have gotten Gentile cooties.) The centurion didn't want Jesus to be put out while doing him a favor.

Instead, the centurion trusted that Jesus' words would be enough: "Only speak a word, and my servant will be healed" (v. 8). His logic is sound. If Jesus was the Word, all he needed to do was speak the word, and the servant will be fine. The creation has no choice but to respond to the Creator.

The centurion's faith astonished Jesus: "When Jesus heard it, He marveled" (v. 10). That's noteworthy, because Jesus was a difficult guy to impress! He continued, "I have not found such great faith, not even in Israel!" Though the centurion was not one of God's people, he demonstrated the behavior—a heart of faith articulated through lips confessing belief in what God can do—that God had sought from the very beginning.

Jesus had never performed a miracle in the way this man was suggesting. Until this point, he had always been physically present when he healed people; he touched them or prayed over them or rubbed mud in their eyes. What the centurion suggested was a long-distance miracle, which suggests a whole other level of faith in Jesus.

Jesus' response to the centurion included three incredible words that held great promise long before they were sung by Paul McCartney and John Lennon: "as you have believed, so *let it be* done for you" (v. 13, emphasis added).

This phrase is actually where we get the word *amen* from. We usually use *amen* at the end of our prayers, as though to say, "May what I have prayed come to pass." But in light of the story of Jesus and the centurion, our goal should be to pray such gutsy prayers that God says *amen* to us.

Faith is the password that unlocks God's power. Jesus said, "If you have faith as a mustard seed, you will say to this mountain, 'Move from here to there,' and it will move; and nothing will be impossible for you" (Matthew 17:20). The Roman soldier had enough faith to ask for a long-distance miracle, and as a result, Jesus granted his request and moved the mountain. He received a miracle because he had faith that made Jesus marvel. Your goal should be to use your words in such a way that they bless the heart of God, inspire faith in those around you, and make life better for those who are hurting.

I Do Like Green Eggs and Ham

Maybe you struggle with being bitter because life has been hard, other people have had it easier, and you feel you would have more rosy things to say if rosier things happened to you. But you don't have to have a lot to do a lot.

Dr. Seuss knew this. He tried to use as few different words as he could when writing. He imposed his own constraints, which liberated him to write better books because he had fewer options. He wrote *The Cat in the Hat* with 236 different words, so his editor bet him he couldn't write a book using only 50 different words. He won the bet when he wrote *Green Eggs and Ham,* one of the bestselling books of all time.

This illustration is even cooler because *Green Eggs and Ham* is about a guy who is anti-everything. He doesn't like anything, and everything is soured by his bad attitude. Only when he tries the thing he thinks he hates does he change his mind-set. When that one thing clicked into place, his whole world changed from negative to positive.

Perhaps you have huge untapped potential but a rebellious spirit that manifests itself in words that are negative and mean, sarcastic and harsh. Could it be that words of humility and submission flowing from a heart that accepts God's sovereignty and his goodness clicking into place could lead to a whole new world of God's using you to do great things, no matter where you go or what you do—whether you are in a boat, with a goat, wearing socks, or with a fox?

It's crazy to think about how much of a difference your attitude can make. Did you know fans have the ability to change the outcome of a sporting event? They can sit there with their arms crossed or open their mouths and cheer. A researcher from Harvard University discovered that crowd noise has a verifiable impact on the game; for every 10,000 fans present, a home team gains an additional 0.1 goal advantage. One person cheering is not so loud, but a whole arena? That's a whole different matter. Expectancy and excitement change everything.

This kind of thinking could change how you show up for church. Theologian William Barclay observed, "There can be no preaching in the wrong atmosphere. Our churches would be different places if congregations would only remember that they preach far more than half the sermon. In an atmosphere of expectancy, the poorest effort can catch fire. In an atmosphere of critical coldness or bland indifference, the most spirit-packed utterance can fall lifeless to the earth."

When your words are full of faith, impossible things can be accomplished. Mountains can move. This doesn't mean there won't be times when you speak words of faith and see nothing happen visibly. In those moments, the most important thing in the world is that you remember that some of God's most important miracles can't be seen with the naked eye. He knows what you need to know: sometimes the mountain that needs moving is inside you.

SOMETIMES
* THE *
MOUNTAIN
THAT NEEDS
MOVING
* IS *
INSIDE YOU

BEING RUDE IS NOT CHEAP

*For every action, there is an
equal and opposite reaction.*

—NEWTON'S THIRD LAW OF MOTION

Hello. My name is Levi Lusko, and I am bad at managing myself.

How about you? Do you ever do things, say things, or tweet things only to realize that what you got is not what you wanted?

I don't want to fight with my wife. I want to laugh with her. I want her to be happy. I want us to have adventures and inside jokes and tickle fights, and get old together like we are a real-life version of the couple in *The Notebook*.

Then why do I act like a jerk, or say things that hurt her feelings, or lose my temper and huff around like a five-foot-ten-and-a-half-inch toddler who hasn't gotten his way? I don't enjoy being in conflict with her. I'd much rather we were making love, or dreaming about the future, or taking a walk, or praying, or eating pasta.

I don't want to fight with my dad. I want to drink coffee with him, work out at the gym with him. Laugh about travel antics. Talk about what we are learning in our walks with God. Reminisce about old stories that make us smile.

Why do I say things that push his buttons? Why do I get defensive and indignant? Why do I put up a wall and refuse to see things through anyone's perspective but my own? It's not because I wanted us to be at a stalemate. I'd prefer we were laughing until one or both of us were crying, or planning a way to get together and have fun.

I don't want to fight with those I work with. I want to work hard with them, not against them. I want our team to be creative, dynamic, and energized. I want our workplace to be challenging but inspiring, a laboratory where we can explore and brainstorm and do things that have never been done before. I want it to be a place where failure isn't disciplined but expected and embraced, so long as it is born of initiative and innovation. I want us to be swept up in passion and excitement and laughter and feel drained but thrilled by the end of the day.

So why do I channel my inner Steve Jobs and become a mercurial, stormy, demanding boss who is a petty dictator, a self-absorbed prig oblivious to the impact my mood, words, and body language have on those around me? I'd much rather my staff were confident in which boss they would get whenever they encountered me, rather than tiptoeing on eggshells until they find out which version of me they are meeting with.

In all these situations, I speak words, make decisions, and

give off nonverbal cues that take me further away from where I actually want to be. If I were to call a time out in any of these moments to think about the implications of my behavior, I would realize this and course-correct. But it often doesn't sink in until Evilevi has already made a mess and left me with the bill.

Dale Carnegie famously said, "If you want to gather honey, don't kick over the beehive." If a bee stings you while you're gathering honey, choosing to respond by kicking the beehive isn't going to help the situation; it's going to make it worse. Instead, a gentle hand will help you get what you want.

Listen to the results of an eye-opening experiment described in the book *Everyday Emotional Intelligence*:

> Participants who were treated rudely by other subjects were 30% less creative than others in the study. They produced 25% fewer ideas, and the ones they did come up with were less original. For example, when asked what to do with a brick, participants who had been treated badly proposed logical but not particularly imaginative activities, such as "build a house," "build a wall," and "build a school." We saw more sparks from participants who had been treated civilly; their suggestions included "sell the brick on eBay," "use it as a goalpost for a street soccer game," "hang it on a museum wall and call it abstract art," and "decorate it like a pet and give it to a kid as a present."

You don't even have to be the recipient of the rough behavior; simply witnessing incivility has negative consequences. The same study showed that "people who'd observed poor behavior performed 20 percent worse on word puzzles than other people did."

The bottom line is that rudeness causes performance and team spirit to deteriorate. There is a cost to being rough. It may get you what feels good in the moment, but it will be at the expense of what you actually want. Being rude is not cheap; it's expensive.

Deep down, you know this. Even while you are sassing your parents, being sarcastic with your spouse, or spouting off at the customer service person who is high on condescension but low on customer service, you know you are making the problem worse—but in those moments, you don't care. You just want to kick the dang beehive.

Soon the situation escalates beyond whatever the original problem was. Instead of dialing down the intensity, you raise it to a whole new level; instead of diffusing the stress, you radiate it back to the source that sent it.

Proverbs 30:32 advises, "If you have been foolish in exalting yourself, or if you have devised evil, put your hand on your mouth." (That right there is some good relationship advice. How much better would your life be if you got better at putting your hand on your mouth?) "For as the churning of milk produces butter, and wringing the nose produces blood, so the forcing of wrath produces strife" (v. 33).

The forcing of wrath in a relationship is, every single time, going to lead to strife. And you're like, *Of course. Ugh, Obvious, right?* And yet, why do we walk away surprised when people's noses are bleeding—ours and theirs—and act mystified as to what happened? *I can't believe it. I can't believe it. I ca—How did this happen?* Oh, I don't know, you were violent and aggressive and mean. And you forced your wrath. But now you don't like the outcome?

Usually in those moments we say to ourselves, *Well, that wasn't my intention*. Right? We use our intentions to excuse what we actually did.

But here's a beautiful, life-changing truth: your intentions don't matter; your behavior does. No one can hear what you *wanted* to say; we hear only what you said. The impact you have on the world is what you're accountable for.

When you allow yourself to be provoked into taking a verbal swing toward someone's nose, you give up the one thing that is yours and yours alone: control of yourself. You see, if I can get to you, I become the boss of you. If I can say the right combination of words or string together enough insults to make you lose your cool and Hulk out, I am effectively in charge, because you've given me the password that unlocks your bad behavior. How many times are you going to let people get your goat before you start locking your goat up in a different place?

I get it. Trust me, I do. I have triggers that have successfully ticked me off so many times it isn't even funny. When I feel unloved or off-kilter or bombarded or out of control, it is almost too easy to allow something to upset me and make words come out of my mouth that I don't want to speak. I feel hypnotized by my hurt feelings, so I fly off in a rage I know I will regret. I have had my emotional passport punched from visiting that territory so many times that I've run out of pages.

I'm sick and tired of handing the reins of my life over to other people and circumstances. But I've found freedom in realizing that regardless of what someone else does, I still have

YOUR
INTENTIONS
— DON'T —
MATTER

YOUR
BEHAVIOR
— DOES —

a choice and can respond in a way that is completely different than my initial impulse. The difference between people and animals is that, because we were made in the image of God, we can choose *not* to do what we feel.

Isn't it time to free yourself from the button pushers in your life?

Four Squares for a Better You

I've come up with a four-part matrix that enables me to slow down when I'm feeling keyed up. It's a graphic that you can copy onto a cocktail napkin, a scrap piece of paper, your journal, or whatever you can get your hands on. I highly recommend that the first few times you use it, you physically draw it and fill it in, because it will force you to cool down. Eventually, you'll be able to do it in your mind in real time, and it will give you the freedom to not say everything you feel like saying.

Draw a cross, and in the top quadrants, from left to right, put the words *Analyze* and *Extrapolate*, leaving a good amount of space below them. In the bottom quadrants, write the words *Prioritize* and *Navigate*.

Under *Analyze*, write: *I want to* . . . and then write exactly what you want to say or do because of being angry, sad, or rejected. Drill down on exactly what you are feeling. Don't run from your emotions; study them.

- *I feel like saying something mean or snarky.*
- *I feel like throwing a tantrum.*
- *I feel like breathing fire on this "customer service"*

person's judgmental self for not helping us even though
we have been waiting longer than anyone.

- *I feel like telling my brother-in-law just what a lazy*
  bum he is.
- *I feel like bringing up ancient history in this argument*
  with my spouse even though it is unrelated and
  off-limits.

As you write down what you want to do, really try to feel the tidal wave pushing you to those behaviors. Don't fight it; just feel it.

Do this every time you feel ready to force your wrath on someone, every time you feel ready to do something that's going to result in strife. Then, stop and analyze what you want to do and why you feel like doing it.

Over time you'll begin to notice common threads, consistent themes, and patterns. You'll notice, every time *this* happens, *this* is how I feel, and *this* is what it makes me want to do. The more we can understand the emotions that drive our words, the better chance we'll have to process them before we act on them.

Analyze your feelings instead of trying to get your aggression out physically. It's better to pick up a piece of paper than it is to hit a pillow, pummel a punching bag, or stab needles into a voodoo doll. Such stress therapy, believe it or not, was once encouraged by experts as a healthy way to get rage out of your system. But in his book on anger, relationship expert Gary Chapman wrote, "Almost all research now indicates that the venting of angry feelings with such aggressive behaviors does not drain a person's anger but actually makes the person more likely to be explosive in the future." The pen is mightier than the stress doll.

After you've analyzed the situation, the next step is to *extrapolate*—if I do *this*, then *this* will happen. Play out the scenario, and take it to its logical end.

In this phase, you're running a simulation, trying on the response before you purchase it and take it out of the store. It's a lifesaver, like having Iron Man's virtual assistant inside your head. The point is to understand the trajectory. You can fly that high, but—just so you know—you don't have enough power in your suit to land safely, Mr. Stark. So go for it if you want, but just know it's going to be a bumpy landing. It's incredibly helpful to understand the implications of a given decision before taking action.

If I say *this*, she will say *that*. If I retort with the perfect insult, it's going to be the shot heard around the world. What's going to happen next? What is he likely to do? What am I then going to do? How will that escalate the situation? What will it do to the tension? What are the long-term impacts on my family, on my kids, on my reputation, on my career?

Just get it all out there. You still can choose to take that course of action—just make sure you do so understanding what will happen next. What dominoes are going to be tipped over by that choice? Proverbs 4:26 says, "Ponder the path of your feet" (ESV). That verse reminds us to ask the question, "Will this path take me to a place I like? Will I enjoy the frosty silence that comes from having responded with a comment that stings?"

A wise person once said, "If you speak when angry, you'll make the best speech you'll ever regret."

The great thing about extrapolating is you can size yourself up and grab the reins of your emotions before they rush you toward a chasm.

The third step is to *prioritize*. Write: *What I really want to happen is. . . .* You played out the implications of what you wanted to do and (I hope) realized that is not what you want to end up with. Now ask, what *do* you want the outcome of this situation to be? How do you want this night to end? If you were to come up with the storyboard for this situation, what's in the last pane of the comic? What is the final scene before the credits roll?

- *I want to be heard.*
- *I want a seat on the plane.*
- *I want respect.*
- *I want to end the night laughing with my wife.*
- *I want to make up so we can make out and then go to sleep cuddling.*

Remember, you originally came for honey, not a bee sting.

When I take the time to do this exercise, I realize that there are things that matter much more than temporary vindication. As good as it feels to unload on someone in the moment, the pleasure is extremely short lived, and you're left with a mess. As I discussed in my last book, *Swipe Right*, don't trade what you want most for what feels good right now.

The last and most important step is to *navigate*. In this quadrant, write: *What I need to do to get there is . . .* What can you do that will get you from where you are to where you want to be? Pro-tip: it will often be the opposite of whatever you started out feeling like doing.

- To get the table at the restaurant you want, try kindness and empathy, not sarcasm and condescension.

- Honesty, humility, and vulnerability work when you want attention from your spouse.
- Calmly telling your sister she hurt your feelings works better than burying the pain deep down and letting it come out through passive aggressive digs.
- Ask people you're in conflict with to help you see the situation through their eyes instead of assuming that your perspective of the event is correct and definitive.

It reminds me of one of Aesop's fables:

One day the Wind and the Sun were disputing which was the stronger. Suddenly they saw a traveller coming down the road, and the Sun said: "I see a way to decide our dispute. Whichever of us can cause that traveller to take off his coat shall be regarded as the stronger[.] You begin." So the Sun retired behind a cloud, and the Wind began to blow as hard as it could upon the traveller. But the harder he blew the more closely did the traveller wrap his coat round him, till at last the Wind had to give up in despair. Then the Sun came out and shone in all his glory upon the traveller, who soon found it too hot to walk with his cloak on.

Kindness effects more than severity.

The wind huffed and puffed but just made the man clench up. The sun lit the day and through gentleness got his way.

The Bible agrees that gentleness and friendliness are stronger than fury and force: "A gentle response defuses anger, but a sharp tongue kindles a temper-fire" (Proverbs 15:1 THE MESSAGE).

Understanding these four steps and applying them has helped my marriage immensely. Our old tendency was to do whatever we would have come up with in quadrant 1. I found that I struggled when we weren't sticking to a plan I had made or something I laid out was not being followed. Then I'd unload a barrage of questions: "Why weren't you ready? Why did you wait to take the girls to the bathroom until the plane was boarding? Didn't you remember I asked you to transfer that money before that check cashed?" I wanted everything to be snappy and happy, punctual and ready to roll, not realizing that no one wants to listen to a petty dictator. It's when you humble yourself as a servant that people want to follow you as a leader. Being nice is one thousand times more effective than being a jerk.

In situations when she was feeling neglected, Jennie used to lock down and pretend everything was fine, but her body language clearly showed she was not happy. What she wants is kindness and affection and attention, but she was trying to get it by acting like a porcupine—and no one wants to hug a porcupine. The best way to get me to care for her is for her to lean in and tell me she is sad and needs me. That breaks my heart and makes me want to embrace her. The other strategy confuses and frustrates me and pushes me away.

Caution: if you choose the productive path instead of the one you originally had in mind, it will feel at first like you're betraying yourself. Our culture places such value on being true to ourselves. Not doing and saying what we feel like is hard because it flies in the face of that concept. But it leads to something even better—becoming who you want to be. My friend Lysa TerKeurst puts it this way in her new book, *It's Not Supposed to Be This Way*: "If we are going to be true to ourselves, we'd better make sure we are being true to our most surrendered, healed, and healthy selves, the ones God made us to be." You might struggle with anger, but you are not an angry person. You were created in the image of God. Those things you feel are not who you really are.

The satisfying sizzle of the smart-alecky remark is like pulling into the Taco Bell drive-through and ordering things covered in nacho cheese when you are starving. The kale salad drizzled sparingly in olive oil—swallowing your pride and doing the right thing—will seem much less pleasing in the moment. How it tastes is not the issue; what it leads to is the key.

I was driving to the airport in Portland from downtown when I realized I was going to miss my flight. The highway was backed up, and there was no end in sight. Waze redirected me to abandon the highway and take surface streets. The route took me through residential neighborhoods with four-way stop after four-way stop. But I didn't care how bizarre it seemed; all that mattered was that it led me to the airport. When you need to get somewhere, the important thing isn't whether a road feels pleasant to drive on. You don't care about the aesthetics of the landscaping or how smooth the asphalt is. All that matters is whether the streets lead to your intended destination. That's the pragmatism you need to apply to the communication in your relationships. It doesn't matter how bumpy the road is; all that matters is, "Will this decision take me where I want to go?" Choosing to abandon the decision to scold, nag, belittle, and criticize will feel so good when you navigate to where you prioritized that you want to be.

Chances are there are situations in which you've been living like Bill Murray in *Groundhog Day*. Again and again, you've ended up in a stalemate or a fight or another frustrating

THOSE
THINGS
YOU FEEL
— ARE NOT —
WHO
YOU
— REALLY —
ARE

encounter with your mother-in-law or your brother, and you've each walked away with blood trickling from noses through forcing your wrath. Perhaps a fresh strategy is in order. "A prudent person sees trouble coming and ducks; a simpleton walks in blindly and is clobbered" (Proverbs 22:3 THE MESSAGE). How many times do you need to get clobbered before you start ducking? Start taking note of the situations that blindside you and incite you to respond in a way you don't like. Then, take note of what they have in common, so you can see them coming and crouch when you need to.

Another helpful question to consider is this: *How would the person I want to be handle this?* You might think that is a little ridiculous, but it helps. I'll think, *What does the Levi I wish I were say to his wife or kids when he is frustrated?* More often than not, the answer is more listening and less speaking, more empathizing and less sermonizing. No one cares what you know if they don't know that you care. When I think it through like that, my choice is easy: *Get thee behind me, Evilevi!*

Picture who you wish you were and imagine that person irritated. Choose to respond as he or she would. Ask God for strength and close the gap between who you are and who you were born to be by making the right choice, regardless of how it feels in the moment.

Change Your Perspective

There is another aspect to keeping your temper in check: knowing that your perspective is not the only one. How you see the situation might not be entirely accurate.

Henry Ford once reflected, "If there is any secret of success, it lies in the ability to get another person's point of view and see things from his angle as well as your own."

It's hard to do that because of the way our brains are built. I read something fascinating in Brené Brown's incredible book *Rising Strong*. She showed convincingly why it can be so difficult to get ourselves into other people's shoes. Apparently when we hear a story, our bodies release cortisol, a stress hormone, that isn't flushed from our system until there is a resolution. She goes on to explain,

> In the absence of data, we will always make up stories. It's how we are wired. In fact, the need to make up a story, especially when we are hurt, is part of our most primitive survival wiring. Meaning making is in our biology, and our default is often to come up with a story that makes sense, feels familiar, and offers us insight into how best to self-protect. . . .
>
> Robert Burton, a neurologist and novelist, explains that our brains reward us with dopamine when we recognize and complete patterns. Stories are patterns. The brain recognizes the familiar beginning-middle-end structure of a story and rewards us for clearing up the ambiguity. Unfortunately, we don't need to be accurate, just certain.
>
> You know that wonderful sensation we experience when we connect the dots or something finally makes sense for the first time? The "*aha* moment," as Oprah calls it? Burton uses that as an example of how we might experience our brain's pattern-recognition reward. The tricky part is that the promise of that sensation can seduce us into shutting down the

uncertainty and vulnerability that are often necessary for getting to the truth.

Burton writes, "Because we are compelled to make stories, we are often compelled to take incomplete stories and run with them." He goes on to say that even with a half story in our minds, "we earn a dopamine 'reward' every time it helps us understand something in our world—even if that explanation is incomplete or wrong."

How crazy is that? Our brains are so hungry to write "case closed" over other people's bizarre behavior that they can cloud us into falsely convicting them of a crime they might not have committed—all to get the satisfaction of not having to wonder what their motives were. Your husband might have been legitimately oblivious, not mean, but because your brain hated not knowing, it played judge, jury, and executioner and determined his motives for him. In Brené's words, you end up feeling certain, even if you aren't accurate. That is a dangerous place to be, because you go on to treat the other person as though they were someone they might not actually be. But because we have already received the chemical reward for our detective work, it's hard for anyone to convince us otherwise. Don't forget that you aren't the only one trying to win the war within. The people in your life might dislike their bad behavior as much as you do. A little patience goes a long way.

It's definitely frustrating when you're on the receiving end of that judgment, when someone seems set in his or her mind about why you did something even though you're trying desperately to set the record straight.

Because of this cognitive bias toward certainty, I remember

being hit super hard when I read the following language Brené recommends in the book: *"The story I am writing in my head" is that you did _____ because you _____. If that is incorrect can you help clear it up for me?* That lets the other person know how you see things and what your brain is trying to make of it, but it sets a soft tone because you haven't yet committed your findings to granite. It gives both of you the chance to see things through each other's eyes.

Using this language in our home has de-escalated so many situations that were increasing in intensity at a fast clip. Jennie and I frequently tell each other the stories our heads are writing and give each other the chance to explain if in fact there is more to the story than meets the eye. Speaking to our daughters in this way and encouraging them to talk to us like this not only defuses situations that otherwise would have continued to escalate but helps them not feel like they're being attacked. The language gives room for the possibility that what you are bringing to their attention might not be the whole truth, and you are humbly asking them to shed light on how you see their actions.

Next time you are feeling flustered because someone said something rude and you want to kick the beehive and let loose a volley of statements so harsh it would make even the saltiest YouTube commenters wince, excuse yourself, draw up a matrix with the four quadrants, and recalculate your route. The more you do it the faster you will get at it, to the point where you can do it in your head in the time it takes to draw in a deep breath. You will need that speed—life is fast and messy, and it only gets crazier when the bullets start flying. Remember—this is war.

I'm going to include a blank quadrant on the next page so you can fill one out with any situation you are dealing with right now. Use this exercise and you'll be able to avoid ordering things that you won't want to pay for when the bill arrives. Being rude might be easy, but it's definitely not cheap.

ANALYZE   EXTRAPOLATE

PRIORITIZE   NAVIGATE

3 ♣

DECLARE
WAR ON

WHAT YOU DO
DECISIONS YOU REPEAT WILL FORM THE LIFE YOU LEAD

3

TAKE BACK THE CONTROLS

R2, get us off this autopilot!
It's gonna get us both killed!

—Anakin Skywalker

Little by little we make our choices, and then our choices make us. The philosopher Will Durant observed, "We are what we repeatedly do." In this section I am going to talk to you about why decisions you repeat are a really big deal.

The robots are taking over. Alexa turns on music and unlocks the front door and sets the alarm. TVs have sensors that detect movement and trigger a painting of your choosing to be displayed on the screen when someone comes in the room. Siri sends text messages for you while you drive, and if you drift as you are fine-tuning your message, the automatic lane assist steers your car back between the dotted lines, and the intelligent braking slows your speed to keep you on pace with the flow of traffic.

LITTLE
— BY —
LITTLE
WE MAKE OUR
CHOICES

* * *

AND THEN
OUR
CHOICES
— MAKE US —

You don't need to know how many teaspoons are in a cup (forty-eight), what the capital of Vermont is (Montpelier), where the hottest place on earth is (Furnace Creek, California) or how old Michael Jackson was when he died (fifty) as long as you can say the words "OK, Google." You never have to tie a string around your finger to remember to order new paper towels or laundry detergent or Nespresso coffee pods when you get to the market or even to your computer or phone; you can push an Amazon Dash button mounted in your kitchen or laundry room, and a thousand miles away a robotic arm grabs what you need from a box with a bar code on the side that it has just scanned. Your items are now on their way.

Why is it that after you have been searching online for yoga pants or Chelsea boots or Lenny Kravitz scarves or hotels in Chicago, every web page you visit is now mysteriously full of ads for yoga pants and Chelsea boots and Lenny Kravitz scarves and hotels in Chicago? You're being studied so you can be marketed to. Your YouTube video likes, your search history, your Facebook posts, the open rates on your emails, the time you spend on websites, how long your mouse hovers before it clicks a link, whether you hesitate before answering a question—all this data is systematically recorded, processed, logged, and commoditized. Companies hope if they show you things you want to see for long enough, you will eventually purchase what they want you to buy.

It's a brave new world overflowing with automation. More and more things happen on their own without the need for human involvement. There are a lot of exciting benefits to these changes. For example, phones automatically switching to Daylight Saving Time takes the stress out of having to remember to do it manually. I also think that cars driving themselves is probably a much better option than people driving them. Flying in an airplane is drastically safer than flying in a car, probably because so much of it is done through autopilot.

I don't tell you this to make you fear the automation happening all around you but to bring to your attention the automation happening *inside* you. It's not just cars and homes and washing machines and websites that have become automated. Your behavior has as well. Your thoughts, your words, how you respond to your moods, what feelings you act on, how you talk to your husband or wife, the way you treat those in authority, and how you speak to yourself are all like water dripping on a rock that eventually wears down a groove. Given enough time, it can become the Grand Canyon.

I came across a fascinating and alarming essay in *Everyday Emotional Intelligence* that claimed that "research suggests that our range of emotional skills is relatively set by our mid-20s and that our accompanying behaviors are, by that time, deep-seated habits." That means the more we act a certain way—happy, depressed, or cranky—the more the behavior becomes engrained in our brain circuitry.

Board-formed concrete is made by pouring concrete into wooden forms, where it will dry and set up. Your habits are like one of those forms, and time is the concrete we pour into it. That means it is absolutely code-blue critical that the wolf rises in your heart and you declare war on the version of you that you don't want to be—you haven't got a moment to lose. You can't afford to put off change until tomorrow; it's now or never. Your habits are hardening as we speak.

Chunking

Your brain seeks to conserve its limited resources in order to have processing power available for what you need. Anything you do repeatedly it seeks to "chunk" together into a routine, a series of steps stored in a file that can be fired off and carried out without your having to think about it. Think about the steps you take when you pour yourself a bowl of cereal. After you pour your milk, you probably always close the refrigerator the same way, whether with your foot or with your left hand. While you're going through this series of motions, you're able to worry about the meeting at work or the email you need to write or whatever you want, because you literally aren't thinking about what you're doing.

Have you ever snapped out of a haze while sitting in your driveway and realized you don't remember anything about the drive home? When you leave work or the gym or the grocery store, your brain says, "I see what's happening. I'll take it from here." This is why the first thing you do when you need to focus on your driving is turn off the radio. As long as you are going through an automated sequence, you can listen to the music, but when you get turned around or encounter a traffic jam, you need to free up brain space so you can actually focus on what you are doing.

You have thousands of these files stored up and sprinkled around the places you go and the situations you regularly find yourself in. If you've ever driven to the wrong place by accident, you've probably ended up somewhere you go frequently, because you mindlessly cued up the wrong file. According to research from Duke University, about 45 percent of our actions each day are habits. That means that close to half of your life you're not actually thinking carefully about what you are doing but are running through an automated ritual baked into your being.

That can be a good thing or a bad thing, depending on what your habits are. Buckling up when you get into your car? Great. Clamming up when you get your feelings hurt? Not so great.

Why were certain files created? Were they because of a bad example? Did you emulate certain behaviors from your family members for so long that they became automated? Perhaps you created files in response to pain. You always drive to Chick-fil-A when you have had a bad day at work because you need empty carbs to take your mind off your feelings. Or you have an alcoholic drink or two at lunch on a workday when you are feeling down.

It's critical to examine what your habits are. Bad habits put you at a decided disadvantage, regardless of what you do the rest of the time. You might have the noblest intentions to honor God or be a person of character, but bad relational, financial, or physical habits can hold you back. If it's true that 45 percent of your life is on autopilot, you are already hamstrung in your attempts to live the life you want, because you are working with only 55 percent of your energy, time, and attention. Based on my napkin math—and keep in mind I am terrible at math—if you made every conscious choice to do right, your highest potential "life grade" is a D once your bad habits are subtracted. It's an enormous handicap to overcome.

On the other hand, if you pour healthy habits into concrete, the right choices become automatic. Whatever conscious effort you put in adds to a good foundation. How epic would it be if, before you used an ounce of willpower and made a single decision, you were starting out at 45 percent? You would only have to give 20 percent effort to be at that same D grade that took three times as much work with bad habits.

Bottom line: you don't have to try nearly as hard if you can get your habits to work for you. Your habits either put the wind in your face or at your back. The right ones need to stay, and the wrong ones need to go.

Distracted from Greatness

One particularly bad habit that threatens our ability to achieve greatness is our addiction to our screens. Americans spend up to five hours a day on our phones. Almost a third of the time we're awake, we're hunched over glowing screens. That's more time given to any other activity in our lives besides sleeping. A hundred and fifty hours a month checking emails, sending texts, playing the newest game, shopping online, putting dog ears and noses on our faces, reading blogs, selecting GIFs and emojis, and catching up on Twitter. Over the course of a lifetime, that adds up to about fourteen years.

Here's a frightening thought: if you have an Instagram account, you are not actually their customer. Have you ever paid them for services rendered? How can you be a customer if you have never bought anything from them? Instagram receives money—you can be sure of that—but not from their users. A customer is one who buys goods or services from a business.

So who is an Instagram customer? Businesses. What does that make you and me? We are the product they are selling. Our eyeballs, to be precise, and little bits of our souls. Instagram gives the app away for free, and once we are on it our attention is sold to those who want to put things in front of us while we are there. We're being used.

60 Minutes ran a special called "Brain Hacking" about how the cell phone industry spends an enormous amount of money to exploit the addictive properties of our electronic devices. Tech companies hire brain experts to figure out how to get us to launch apps more frequently and spend more time (and money) on them—in other words, to make their use a habit. "Likes," texts, notifications, and emails trigger dopamine rewards in our brains, and we feel the same pleasure that comes from pulling a slot machine in a Las Vegas casino. Checking your phone or tablet is the equivalent of yanking the slot machine arm, because your mind is eager to see what is going to come next. When you haven't touched your device in a while, your brain releases a stress hormone called cortisol in a plot to trigger another hit of dopamine, and you feel afraid you might be missing out on something. Justin Resenstein, the man who created the Facebook "like" button, now describes likes as "bright dings of pseudo-pleasure."

On that episode of *60 Minutes,* Anderson Cooper interrupted the expert he was interviewing to say he couldn't focus on the conversation because all he could think about was whether he had gotten a text. The researchers hooked him up to electrodes and put his phone out of sight; the needle jumped when Cooper's phone buzzed and he couldn't answer it. You could literally see the FOMO and PSA (phone separation anxiety) on the display coming from his brain! It's unfortunate but true: the conditioned response of compulsively refreshing our email inboxes or messages or social accounts doesn't satisfy you. It only deepens your dependence and leaves you like an alcoholic craving another drink.

The experts admitted to such practices as holding back likes until a time when the algorithms indicate you are most likely to spend a good period of time on the device. That's why you won't get just one like but a burst of them. It's all to turn your mind to mush.

And it's working.

The robots are taking over, all right—only *we* are the robots, jumping every time the ping sounds and drooling every time the bell rings. How are you ever going to do all the great things God has called you to do if you give away that much control of yourself?

I recently read David McCullough's *The American Spirit: Who We Are and What We Stand For*, and it stopped me dead in my tracks. McCullough is a celebrated historian whose bestsellers on subjects like the Revolutionary War, President John Adams, and the Wright brothers are all incredible reads. *The American Spirit*, however, is a collection of speeches he has given at college graduations and notable occasions like the two-hundredth anniversary of the building of the White House.

His words shook me, especially when he talked about the fact that so many people today don't read. Among those with a college degree, a third didn't read a single book last year. Staggering! (If you have made it this far, you are probably going to finish, so yay, you!)

One part in particular that gave me pause was his description of Thomas Jefferson: "He read seven languages. He was a lawyer, surveyor, ardent meteorologist, botanist, agronomist, archaeologist, paleontologist, Indian ethnologist, classicist, brilliant architect. Music, he said, was the passion of his soul, mathematics, the passion of his mind."

Are you kidding me? Seven languages? A meteorologist? Indian ethnologist? Architect? But don't pay any attention to that because music was his real passion—of his soul, anyway. In his mind, he was always a math guy. I read that paragraph out loud to Jennie and remarked, "This is why he was able to write the Declaration of Independence." Which, by the way, he wrote at age thirty-three.

Imagine sitting down, the entire Continental Congress breathing down your neck and George Washington waiting to cross the Potomac, and writing these words: "We hold these truths to be self-evident, that all men are created equal, that they are endowed by their Creator with certain unalienable Rights, that among these are Life, Liberty and the pursuit of Happiness."

If you put down your phone for a few minutes, picked up books a little more, and took up a hobby like paleontology or botany—or, heck, why not both and six more—perhaps you, too, would be capable of creating something that could change the world.

The world doesn't need another Declaration of Independence, but it does desperately need to see the greatness Jesus has given you—greatness that is bursting to come out. But you have to win the war with yourself before it can ever see the light of day.

The habits you allow in your life today are going to determine who you become tomorrow.

Future you is an exaggerated version of current you. Time doesn't change anything; it merely deepens and reveals who we are. If you are kind today, you will be kinder tomorrow. If you are cruel today, that, too, will deepen. Smile lines or frowning wrinkles are forming on your face at this very moment. Generous old people are people who, when they were young, lived lives of generosity, and cranky old people grew out of young people who never learned to get out of their own way.

At a commencement speech David McCullough spoke to a generation that is addicted to the Internet and has lost sight of simple pleasures:

"Sometime, somewhere along the line, memorize a poem. Sometime, somewhere along the line, go out in a field and paint a picture, for your own pleasure. Sometime, somewhere along the line, plant a tree, buy your father a good bottle of New York state wine, write your mother a letter."

Whatever new habits you decide on, make sure to write them down. Those who commit their goals to paper are 42 percent more likely to accomplish them and earn nine times as much over their lifetimes as people who don't.

As we make our way into the next chapter, where I'm going to talk more about how to weed your habit-garden, know this: it will feel really uncomfortable to jettison behavior that has been with you for a long time. Your desire for comfort will beg you to go back to how it used to be. But you mustn't relent from what you wrote down at the beginning of the book, when you chose to declare war. I'm begging you.

THE HABITS
YOU
ALLOW
★ IN YOUR ★
LIFE
— TODAY —
ARE GOING
TO
DETERMINE
★ WHO YOU ★
BECOME
TOMORROW

People who die of hypothermia are often found naked. In their final moments, they were convinced they were hot, so they shed their clothes.

What feels right and what is right are two very different things.

START BEFORE YOU'RE READY

The way to get started is to quit
talking and begin doing.

—WALT DISNEY

We are in it now, you and I. I salute you for making it this far. That means you are serious about bettering yourself enough to have soldiered on to chapter 9 in a book called *I Declare War*, and you haven't dropped out like a Navy SEAL wannabe who rings the bell during Hell Week. Bravo! There is more of the book in your left hand than your right hand, less swiping in front of you than behind you. If you are listening to the audiobook, I have fewer words to say than I have said.

In the first section, we laid down the first card as we discovered the importance of the thoughts we think. With the second card, we explored the words we speak. Now, with the third card, we're working through the things we do—our actions, the daily choices that over time become cemented into habits. I hope the previous chapter opened your eyes to how serious this subject is, because our brains are eager to harden our daily choices into our destinies. There is no such thing as a small decision.

Every time you make a decision, it's like a domino falling over—and everyone knows that one domino takes down the next. A physicist named Hans van Leeuwen discovered that every time a domino falls, it generates a force sufficient to knock down a domino twice as big as itself. That means that in decisions, as in dominoes, we have a phenomenally powerful force on our hands. One choice affects another, and the effects of those choices accumulate and magnify over time. This is called *exponential growth*.

I came across a fascinating legend about the invention of chess in sixth-century India. Supposedly the inventor who brought it to the king for his approval found that the monarch loved it. The king found this miniature war to be a challenging and puzzling battle of wits and was delighted with it. He rather bombastically told the inventor that he could name his reward, fully expecting him to ask for a bag of gold, land holdings, or perhaps a title.

Instead, with one hand the man reached into a bowl of food on the table and grabbed a handful of grains, and with the other he swept the pieces from the chess board that separated them. Placing one grain on a single square in one of the corners and then two on the second square, he said, "For my reward, I would like to be given grain sufficient to cover this board in this fashion. The third will have twice what is on the second, and so on until all the spaces are filled."

THERE IS NO
SUCH
THING
— AS A —
SMALL
DECISION

The king was incredulous and, full of pity, he pressed whether the inventor wouldn't prefer a fancy home or expensive horse. When the man indicated that all he wanted was the grain, the king slapped him on the back and decreed that it would be done.

When the inventor departed, the king told the servants to fill the board with food and have it sent to the inventor's home. But once the math was calculated a trembling attendant brought to the king his notes. There was not enough money in the entire kingdom to finance this debt nor enough grain in all of India to accomplish it. In fact if the entire surface of the earth were covered in a layer of grain, it would need to be twice as big in order to equal the amount of grain required. How did the sum get so big? The grains of rice compounded one space at a time, and soon it was checkmate.

Another illustration is even crazier: if you attempt to fold a single sheet of paper in half multiple times, you won't be able to fold it more than seven or eight times. *MythBusters* proved that you can go as high as eleven, but their paper was the size of a football field, and they used a forklift and steamroller to fold it inside Kennedy Space Center, so I'm not sure it counts. The world record number of folds stands at twelve, accomplished by a teenager who used toilet paper for the experiment.

Folding paper also shows the power of compounding, because every time you fold the pages it doubles in thickness. First you have one page, but after folding you have two; a fourth fold makes sixteen pages, and on it goes, doubling and doubling and doubling. If you could keep up this progression, by the time you got to twenty-three folds your stack of pages would be a kilometer high.

Thirty folds? It would reach a hundred kilometers, which is the beginning of outer space.

Forty-two folds? To the moon.

Fifty-one? Your stack of paper is now *en fuego*, because it has reached the sun.

And if you could somehow hit 103 folds, the stack that started as a single sheet of paper would measure 93 billion light years from end to end, stretching across the boundaries of the known universe.

Understanding the mind-boggling phenomenon of exponential growth has the capacity to change every aspect of your life. It's the difference between 17 percent interest on $97,700 in credit card debt and 17 percent interest on that same amount tucked away in a 401k ($16,609, in black ink or in red ink). It's the gap between eating a hundred fewer calories and a hundred more calories than you burn each day for a year (a staggering twenty-pound difference, which is pretty wild considering a hundred calories isn't even half of a Snickers bar). And that is just in a single year; carried out over a longer period, the results diverge even more. In the time it takes for a single decade to come and go, you can end up massively in debt or a hundred pounds overweight and struggling to control your diabetes—or you can be healthy, have energy, and enjoy financial prosperity that puts you in a place to be the one helping other people. C. S. Lewis elaborated on this idea in his classic *Mere Christianity*:

> Good and evil both increase at compound interest. That is why the little decisions you and I make every day are of such infinite importance. The smallest good act today is the capture of a strategic point from which, a few months later,

you may be able to go on to victories you never dreamed of.
And apparently trivial indulgence in lust or anger today is
the loss of a ridge, a railway line or bridgehead from which
the enemy may launch an attack otherwise impossible.

It is critical that you take seriously the battles you are facing. It might feel like a small thing that you get in fights with
your parents that cause you to fly off the handle or that you
can't control your anger when provoked by your sister, but
if you can't keep your temper in check, down the road you'll
be in an adversarial relationship with your boss where you
fly off the handle or a marriage where you can't control your
anger. The stakes get bigger; the stimuli do not. When you
once stormed into your room and slammed the door, you now
run back to your parents' house or sleep over on a best friend's
couch. Instead of an earlier curfew or getting grounded, now
you're unemployed or in a messy divorce. A lack of self-control
now sets the stage for a future in which your emotions get the
best of you. It won't be easier to win the war within when you
grow up on the outside if you never did on the inside.

There is no such thing as an unimportant chess piece. The
queen seems more important than the pawns, but what you do
in the early stages of the game are just as important as how you
handle the fancier pieces once they come into play many moves
in. The sooner you can discover this, the better off you'll be.

Paul told Timothy to not let other people despise his youth
but to set an example (1 Timothy 4:12). We can be just as guilty
of not taking our young selves seriously. A note for my younger
readers: what you're doing now matters. You are putting habits into motion while you are in high school and college that

are going to hurt or help you down the road, especially if you decide to get married. To go back to the chess metaphor, by the time the king and queen—the married chess pieces—come into play, they are either helped or hurt by what the other pieces did earlier in the game. You might be in the knight or bishop or rook stage of life now, but those matter just as much as what the king and queen do.

If you buy something online every time you get stressed out or feel bored or lonely, you are only numbing your feelings with a quick hit of happiness instead of facing them. The Amazon boxes will pile up in your garage, but the real problem will still be there, deep down, and it will only get worse, and not better, with time. You need to learn to feel your feelings—lean into them, diagnose them, and then do what is needed to move through them. Distracting yourself with meaningless activity or spending or entertainment when you are blue will become a pattern you get entrenched in, and it will only ever lead to a heightened discontent. If instead you can learn now to lean into the discontent you are tempted to medicate or run from, and try to understand what is driving it, you can look to the Lord to fill the hole instead of the shiny trinkets and baubles of this world you would otherwise turn to. You will discover that the ache you were going to silence with something from iTunes or something made from cashmere was actually the voice of Jesus calling you to himself. It's a gift to be unsettled and unsatisfied, because it is in those moments we can potentially find what we truly need in him. The silencing of that discomfort by fast food or fast delivery from e-commerce is more punishment than it is reward.

I've discovered that when I'm feeling low, it's usually

because of something that has very little to do with the way the problem is visible. Crabbiness toward someone at work or Jennie or the kids is caused by something deeper than what is happening in the moment. It's never explained just by how it is manifesting. When all I can see is everyone else's faults, it's because projecting my bad behavior functions as armor to protect me from dealing with what I really need to face in my heart.

In fact, in the space of time that it has taken to write this chapter, I had three different situations that were frustrating and upsetting to me. What I realized was that I was anxious about finishing this book on time, and instead of dealing with that, I was lashing out and not giving the kindness and gentleness to those around me that they deserve. That's the downside of writing a book telling you how to face your demons—it leaves me no choice but to face mine.

It's easier than you think to become set in your ways. Fortunately, that's true for good and not just for evil. People talk about going through the motions as though that were a bad thing, but it's only bad if you're going through the *wrong* motions. Choosing to be vulnerable and opening up when you feel like shutting down, starting with God when you feel like rushing into the business of the day, listening when you feel like speaking, thinking when you feel like acting, and taking the time to put yourself in other people's shoes and see the situation through their eyes when you are already certain you know the whole story—these habits can get locked into your muscle memory too. You can get compound interest on good *and* evil.

An old proverb says the best time to plant a tree is twenty years ago, but the second-best time is right now. It would have been great if your parents had taught you how to process your emotions in a healthy way. Ideally you never would have been sexually assaulted by your brother's friend, and you never would have carried shame and trauma that caused you to wear masks. In a perfect world, you wouldn't have fifteen years of throwing a tantrum when you don't get your way baked into your muscle memory. I sure wish I could take back the thousands of times I shot off my mouth without thinking about the consequences, a response that got locked into my reflexes one fold of paper at a time. You can't go back and change the past, but what you can do is plant a new tree of good behavior right now. Twenty years from now you will be glad you did.

The right time to do the right thing is right now. Every second you stall is time that exponential growth could be working its slow magic.

If you choose to delay until tomorrow what you should be doing today, you forfeit the opportunity to power through the necessary humble beginnings for another precious twenty-four hours. There is not a moment to lose. You get into and out of things the same way: one step at a time.

Flip the Switch

It's not getting to the finish line that is the most difficult part of any journey or undertaking; it's showing up at the starting line. The dread of beginning is unbearable. The space shuttle uses more fuel taking off than in the rest of the flight put together. The hardest part is getting off the ground.

I procrastinated starting to write this book. For months, I

YOU GET
INTO AND
OUT OF
THINGS THE
SAME
— WAY —
ONE STEP
AT A
TIME

thought about it and thought about it and kept telling myself I was going to begin, but fear crept in and I would psyche myself out. It was the same way for *Through the Eyes of a Lion* and for *Swipe Right*. But once I ripped off the Band-Aid and started typing, an amazing thing happened—I gained momentum. I believe you will have the same experience as you decide to start slapping your cards on the table and declare your own war.

Legendary football coach Vince Lombardi described what I am saying: "A man can be as great as he wants to be. If you believe in yourself and have the courage, the determination, the dedication, the competitive drive, and if you are willing to sacrifice the little things in life and pay the price for the things that are worthwhile, it can be done." He also observed, "Once a man has made a commitment to a way of life, he puts the greatest strength in the world behind him. It's something we call heart power. Once a man has made this commitment, nothing will stop him short of success." Finally, he quipped, "The harder you work, the harder it is to surrender."

It's simple physics, really. Unless acted on by an outside force, objects at rest stay at rest and objects in motion stay in motion. At least that's my recollection of Sir Isaac Newton's brilliant discovery as he articulated it in the First Law of Motion. The hardest part is disrupting inertia. Once you put a new habit into motion, you'll feel the wind at your back. I'm not minimizing how hard inertia is to overcome; I'm just reassuring you that, as Teddy Roosevelt discovered, there is a prize waiting for you on the other side of the barbed wire—the wolf will rise.

You mustn't overthink the decision or you will talk yourself out of what you need to do. Overanalysis leads to paralysis. I finally got so fed up waiting for myself to feel ready to start writing that I simply took the plunge. Bernard Roth describes this as flipping an internal switch:

> Whenever anyone makes an important change, it's because a switch has flipped. Someone who has struggled her whole life with her weight finally decides to get fit. Someone who has put up with an abusive boss for years finally has enough and quits. Someone who has harbored a secret crush finally takes the plunge and asks her beloved out for coffee. A shift has happened that has made action favorable to inaction.

When you have chosen enough times to zig when you normally would have zagged, zigging will become your new normal. Objects in motion tend to stay in motion. As the brilliant researcher Charles Duhigg pointed out, habits we already have locked into place can't be deleted, but they can be overwritten. Once created, a file will always be there, but what happens when it gets triggered can be modified. He explains that a habit is essentially a loop comprised of a *cue*, a *routine*, and a *reward*. In his book *The Power of Habit*, he claimed, "If you can break a habit into its components, you can fiddle with the gears. . . . Almost any behavior can be transformed if the cue and reward stay the same."

The only difference between a noose and a lasso is which end of the rope you are at. When you switch out the *routine*— the middle part of the habit loop—on your bad habits, you can change your life, transforming what is harming you into a weapon that can help you destroy your alter ego and move you closer to becoming who you want to be.

The first few times—and maybe even the first thousand times—you respond to the old cue in a new way won't be easy. Full disclosure: it might feel unbearable. But do it long enough and you will be only a little uncomfortable. Eventually you'll feel unstoppable. When you commit yourself to the process, you'll feel like David when he exclaimed, "With your help I can advance against a troop; with my God I can scale a wall" (Psalm 18:29 NIV).

The journey of a million miles has to start somewhere, and that somewhere is where you plant your shoe on the ground for the first time and believe that providence will have your back.

THE GAME BEFORE THE GAME

All men are created equal. Some
just work harder in the preseason.

—Reebok commercial
featuring Emmitt Smith

Out of all the many good repeated decisions you need to make room for in your life (tithing, flossing, staying physically fit, eating well, spending less than you earn, and so on), what I'm going to tell you in this chapter has been the biggest game changer for me: the concept of intense preparation so that you can effortlessly enjoy the actual competition. I'm going to give you some super simple handles so you can show up for life at your best. These same things that will help you ramp up for high-stakes situations can be used to catch yourself when you are slipping. But first, a story.

At one of the biggest speaking engagements of my life, I

peed on myself moments before going on stage. Yeah, proud moment for sure.

I knew I had to be on in five. With all that was going on in my head, I didn't realize until it was too late that I really wouldn't be comfortable through the message if I didn't go to the bathroom. It was dicey, but I decided to make a run for it. I turned off my mic pack as I made my way to the ready room that had been set up for me about fifty yards away. The last thing I needed was for the mic to get turned on and for thousands of people to listen to me go to the bathroom.

Between trying to go over my message in my head, racing the ticking clock telling me I had to be center stage when the song ended, and my attempts to manage the logistics of the process, everything went wrong. The weight of the mic pack pulled my entire belt off backward mid-stream. When I lunged for the belt to keep it from landing on the floor and pulling out the microphone cord that was snaking up my shirt, I lost control of the situation. Now, 9,999 times out of 10,000, taking a leak is a simple and straightforward affair, so this was a noteworthy anomaly in my life.

(For the record, I want to admit that women have a thousand times more complications than men when it comes to bathroom dynamics, from the lines to get in the stall to the fact that standing up at a urinal is simply not an option—and I have no clue how one would go about it in a romper. My deepest respect goes out to all of you who must sit, especially when it comes to the foulest of locations. This sympathy is not lip-service at all; as a father to four daughters, I have held small, squirming bodies six inches above toilets from Louisiana to London, even after putting on seat covers or thirteen layers of toilet paper, in order to avoid delicate contact with disgusting surfaces.)

Anyway, the situation was a train wreck. By the time the dust settled, I had caught the mic pack but managed to wet my pants. It takes a special kind of person to pee his pants while going to the bathroom. What can I say? I have a gift.

Fortunately, I was wearing dark pants, and you couldn't really tell that they were wet. (*Keep telling yourself that, buddy.*) I tried pitifully to rinse it off, then used several squirts of Purell to sanitize everything. After some quick pats with a paper towel, I was out of time. I sprinted back to the stage and grabbed my Bible. At that moment the song ended, and I had to take the stage.

People ask me, "How do you stay humble while traveling around speaking to thousands of people?" I often think of this particular moment when that question is asked, because the audience that day saw only what happened in the spotlight. I have a backstage pass to my life and know that the guy under those bright lights was wearing wet pants.

I was relieved (pun intentional) to discover that I'm not the only one who has had a big day dampened by a full bladder. On May 5, 1961, Alan Shepard piloted the first American manned space flight in history. As the first astronaut of the Mercury 7 chosen to follow in the footsteps of the chimpanzees launched by NASA, he instantly became one of the most famous people in the nation and was celebrated around the country like David was when he went up against Goliath as a single combat warrior. And yet, in the midst of his big day, he experienced an unceremonious bathroom event. The flight was only supposed to last fifteen minutes, so no one thought of adding a urine receptacle to the flight suit. After he was strapped into the tiny capsule, there were delays due to weather and an overheating inverter, so he was stuck on his back facing the sky for four hours with no way to do anything about the mounting crisis building up in his bladder.

In our day, rocket launches don't even make the news. *Oh, they did that again? Yawn. Tweet me when Matt Damon lands on Mars.* But on that day, on live TV from coast to coast, unbroken news coverage showed the Redstone rocket sitting on the launch pad as viewers with glistening eyes watched spellbound. Half the newspapers in America had reporters at his home, tearing up his lawn, and craning their necks to get a glimpse of his family inside watching the launch on TV. Highway patrolmen reported that drivers all across the country had pulled over to the shoulders of highways and boulevards because they were so nervous while listening to the coverage live on AM radio that they couldn't drive. The country was beside themselves as they collectively wondered, *What is going through this man's mind as he sits there hanging his hide out over the edge in an eight-story-high bullet on top of a 66,000-pound rocket waiting to be blasted into the heavens?* Truth be told, all he was thinking about was how bad he had to pee.

He held out as long as he could without telling Mission Control about his predicament for fear that the launch would be scrubbed. His mission had already been postponed because of weather, and he refused to be the astronaut who didn't fly because of a potty emergency!

When he finally broke the news to the tower and asked permission to relieve himself in his suit, NASA's finest deliberated over it for some time. The biggest concern was that the sudden introduction of liquid would cause his suit's monitoring systems and his cooling system to malfunction.

The book *The Right Stuff* describes the moment when he finally receives permission:

> Finally they told him to go ahead and "do it in the suit." And he did. Because his seat, or couch, was angled back slightly, the flood headed north, toward his head, carrying consternation with it. The flood set off a suit thermometer, and the Freon flow jumped from 30 to 45. On swept the flood until it hit his chest sensor, which was being used to record his electrocardiogram, and it knocked that sensor out partially, and the doctors were nonplussed. . . . The wave rolled on . . . finally pooling in the valley up the middle of Shepard's back.

When the now larger-than-life Shepard arrived back on Earth, he was met by the president and first lady. He enjoyed a ticker tape parade in New York City and free drinks at bars everywhere he went for years to come. A hundred reporters asked him about his experience, and each time he would smile and speak of the great new era of space travel and the honor of doing his duty for a country locked in a space race. I'm sure part of him snickered on the inside thinking about the behind-the-scenes fact that, as he soared through the heavens powered by thousands of pounds of exploding liquid oxygen, he did so drenched in his own urine.

You can see why it is a mistake to rush to judge a situation based on limited information. People often assume someone who makes their living in front of people must be fighting a battle with ego, when in reality they might be fighting a very different struggle you know nothing about. I'm not saying the whole "how do you keep yourself humble" question isn't important; pride is sinister and deadly. It is the sin that Satan first fell prey to (Isaiah 14:12–17) and summarily was responsible for every sin that followed. If something split heaven and started hell I think it deserves a healthy fear. However, the question presupposes that the automatic reaction to any kind of public attention is going to be thoughts of self-exaltation.

I have found the exact opposite to be true. The first thought to go through my head when God does anything great through my life is, *Who am I that you would use me?* I know myself. The vast majority of my life is not spent on a stage. Even if I gave a public address every single day, which in even the busiest seasons I wouldn't think of scheduling, I would still have twenty-three hours every day *not* speaking into a microphone.

No matter what God does for any of us, the real bulk of our lives is made of unglamorous, unsexy, unspectacular opportunities to keep our eyes on Jesus (or not), press through anxious thoughts and worries (or not), and demonstrate perseverance and passion (or not) in the trenches of daily life. That's what I want to talk to you about in this chapter—not what happens on the court or the field of the stadium, where the cameras are recording and the crowds are cheering, but what you go through during the drive to the stadium, what happens in your head in the locker room, and how you feel at 4:00 a.m. when your alarm goes off and more than anything in the world you *don't* want to get up and practice. I want to talk about the game before the game.

If you look at someone excelling in their craft and doing

THE REAL BULK
OF OUR
LIVES IS MADE
— OF —
UNGLAMOROUS
UNSEXY
UNSPECTACULAR
OPPORTUNITIES
✦
TO KEEP
OUR EYES
ON JESUS

something impossible—be it a figure skater, a freestyle rapper, or an ice sculptor—and you watch them perform for five minutes, remember that you are probably looking at a few thousand hours of work for every one of those eye-dazzling minutes. The work they do ahead of time gives them success when the cameras are rolling and the teddy bears are being thrown onto the ice.

Twenty years ago, I volunteered to set up chairs so that someone else could preach sermons. Fifteen years ago, I was putting the exact same amount of work I give now to create messages to speak to a group of high school students. I remember when Fresh Life had only a few dozen people sitting in the rows, but I agonized over my sermons, spending early morning and late night hours to make sure they were perfect. The number of people listening to what I have to say might have changed, but what I am saying and why I am saying it has not.

While cleaning out a closet in our house, Jennie and I stumbled upon a collection of my old sermon notes from when I first began preaching. Each one had thousands of words, first handwritten, then typed out and tweaked with pen in the final few minutes. In the earliest days I would actually pace around and record the message into a little handheld tape recorder and play it back so I could hear how it was going to sound. If I didn't like it, I'd start all over again. These days I don't record the sermon in advance, but the preparation process still has multiple steps, including hand-writing the message from the typed notes so I can memorize what I am going to say.

Looking at those old materials, I was transported back sixteen years in time to the days when I would get physically sick before taking the stage. I relate to Eminem puking in the bathroom of the club before his first hip-hop battle in *8 Mile*. It wasn't because of my mother's spaghetti (I could never preach with something that heavy and rich in my stomach), but for a year or so, I would almost always end up dry-heaving before speaking.

In those days, I was tortured by the whole process of gearing up to speak. I would feel shaky, light-headed, and absolutely terrified that I would go blank as I tried to remember the key points of my message. Sometimes the anxiety set in as early as twenty-four hours ahead of time, especially before a bigger speaking engagement. Once I was asked to speak at a concert in an amusement park where there could be as many as a thousand people listening. I was so terrified by the pressure that I woke up with night sweats and fear every hour on the hour the entire night before the event.

I usually felt better after throwing up. I didn't ever have private preparation space in those days, so I would resort to wherever I could find. An alley behind the building, a public restroom, a closet, whatever was available. But I always felt fine the moment I took the stage. All the jitters dissipated, and I felt like a duck in water, doing what I was born to do. It was just agony to get there.

Here's the deal: the bridge between all that practice and the performance is the pregame routine. If you're not familiar with athletics you might think of locker rooms as those smelly places where people who play sports change. Not so. The locker room is a sacred space where a warrior puts his or her game face on. The same is true in nearly every endeavor. You have to win the war inside before you can win the war outside.

GROW YOUR GRIT

There have been studies done as to what type of person makes it through Navy SEAL training and Hell Week. It's not necessarily the best athletes who succeed; it is those with "grit." In SEAL-speak, *grit* means mental toughness. Physical limits are actually determined by mental limits.

Nothing has helped me to do what I do better than learning to intentionally build my grit—the mental toughness of spirit that comes from crossing the barbed wire again and again—so I can move toward the best version of myself on stage, in my home, and in the office. Looking back on the twenty-year-old version of myself puking in the alley behind an amusement park, I see that I was doing so many things that were counterproductive. I was actually enhancing the jitters, pouring fire on my fear, and making myself *more* susceptible to my nerves instead of embracing the powerful feelings and putting a saddle on the energy so I could ride it. Having butterflies in your stomach isn't the end of the world; you just gotta whip those butterflies into formation so they fly in the right direction!

Here are some tips for developing your grit and getting yourself ready for what is in front of you. These principles don't just help with public speaking; they'll help you in a job interview, football game, piano recital, sales pitch, or any other occasion where you feel anxious.

1. BREATHE DEEPLY.

Did you know that 20 percent of all oxygen you breathe goes straight to the brain? Your body's priority is to keep you alive, and it's always going to dedicate and divert the bulk of oxygen coming in to critical lifesaving functions. Analytics and emotional processing will always take a backseat to other things. So if you're breathing shallowly, the result is a loss of memory, a loss of focus, and a loss of power to overcome your moods. It also brings a heightened sense of anxiety and depression. Shallow breaths are terrible for you.

Of course, the more nervous you get, the more you are tempted to take shallow breaths, but that is when you need to breathe more than ever.

Using your mind correctly becomes increasingly more challenging as your heart beats faster. In his book *10-minute Toughness: The Mental Training Program for Winning Before the Game Begins*, Jason Selk explains that when your heart is beating at about 120 beats per minute, you will not be nearly as sharp; by 150 beats per minute, your mind basically shuts down. As pressure escalates, you become more tempted to breathe faster and shallower, but this is when you need oxygen like never before. Sometimes when I memorize something, I'll practice saying it while I do jumping jacks or high knees to see if I can still recite it with my heart rate elevated.

I've been practicing deep breathing for a few years now, because inevitably here's what happens: the program organizer will say, "Hey, you had forty-five minutes, but someone went long, so now you've got twenty-five." And I'm thinking, *Which half of my message do I give?*

And then the organizer continues, "And make sure at the end you say this . . . and whatever you do, don't say that . . ." And I'm like, *Ugh.*

Then I'll get a text, right at that moment, maybe something from someone on our staff. "So and so quit" or "We're getting sued" or "The roof on the building is leaking and it will cost thirty grand to fix it" or "The construction estimate was wrong and the schedule is delayed."

And in the midst of all this, I am supposed to get up to speak?

I can feel myself getting nervous and my pulse quickening. Often I will even be holding my breath. So though it's counterintuitive, I immediately take a big, deep, and ultra-slow breath. The less I feel like doing it, the more I know I need it. I've heard different numbers, but fifteen seconds is a good one to shoot for, with a formula of 6-2-7: breathing in for six seconds, holding it for two, and then out for seven seconds. If the breath doesn't cause your stomach to bulge out you are not going deep enough.

My boxing coach makes me do the same thing when we are working on conditioning. After a minute of all-out burpees or thirty seconds of blasting the heavy bag as fast as I can as many times as possible, my heart is thundering to where I feel like I am going to die. My coach always reminds me to take deep, slow breaths, because my instinct is to match my breaths to my heartbeats. But those deep, slow breaths are what I need, despite how they feel.

When I find myself freaking out moments from taking the stage, and I take a deep breath, I can actually feel myself calm down. I picture all the oxygen flooding my brain, and more and more of it coming back to life.

Deep breathing is also a good thing to do when you find yourself angry in a meeting or escalating into an argument with your spouse. You can't say something you will regret later while you are breathing deeply.

2. THINK ABOUT YOUR POSTURE.

If you haven't seen Amy Cuddy's TED talk titled "Your Body Language May Shape Who You Are," you should check it out. It's one of the most watched TED talks of all time, and it went so viral that the content also became a *New York Times* bestselling book. You probably know that much of what you communicate to people when you speak comes through nonverbally. But Cuddy shows compellingly how much of an impact your body language has on you. Nervous energy usually causes you to hunch over, tuck your chin, put your hands on your neck, or cross your arms. But that cascades into more nervousness because of the release of cortisol (stress) into your system.

However, putting your hands on your hips, like Wonder Woman, or up in the air, is the universal sign of victory and celebration. (Picture someone who has just scored a touchdown or aced a test.) When you do this your body releases testosterone and your levels of cortisol drop by as much as 25 percent. This can happen in as little as 120 seconds.

I was completely shocked when I initially watched this video, but the first thing I thought of was the book of Psalms. It is full of commands to praise God with raised hands and heads held high. You can't find a psalm that tells you to tuck yourself into a ball and sing to God meekly with your hands in your pockets. It's all about shouting with a voice of triumph. Could it be that part of the reason God wants you to shout and sing triumphantly with your arms in the air isn't just because of what you are declaring about him but because of what happens to you when you obey? He gives you feelings to match what is coming from your lips and modeled with your body. It's also no mistake that the average song lasts around three to five minutes, so singing with your hands up will put you in that position for much more than the needed two minutes.

That's one of the many reasons why you will not find me backstage during the worship set before I speak as I was in my early days. I need the time worshiping through song more than I need a few more minutes cramming. You can't be a wolf if you won't lift up your voice and howl. And spiritual benefits aside, it's a natural opportunity to change from the mousy posture of nervous preparation to a dominant stance of victory and strength.

3. YOUR FACIAL EXPRESSIONS MATTER.

What does your face look like right now as you read this? Is your brow furrowed in concentration? When Jennie sees me deep in thought while reading emails that she can tell upset me, she will often smooth out the skin between my eyes right above the bridge of my nose. She rubs the crease away with her thumb and smiles at me as though to say, *Lighten up, buddy.* She is giving good advice—in terms of both what kind of response you radiate and what you will receive in response.

Researchers have found that people respond in kind to the facial expressions they encounter. A smile is met with a smile, and a frown with a frown. This mirroring happens subconsciously. We instinctively reflect what we see. If you want people around you to cheer up there is something you can do about that. Seeing someone display facial expressions of fear, anger, sadness, or disgust causes an increased heart rate, elevated skin temperature, and sweating. Your face can absolutely have an impact on those around you, for better or worse.

Your face also affects your own mood. Throwing on a large smile to the point where your cheeks go up causes your mind to feel the emotion you have on your face.

In a study in France, researchers had two groups of people read newspaper comics. One group did so normally, and the others were asked to read the same comics while holding a pencil sideways clenched between their teeth. Holding the pencil this way activates the same muscles in the cheek that are used in flashing a broad smile. When interviewed afterward, those who read the comics while smiling all found the cartoons to be far more humorous, and they had a better time reading them than those without the pencils in their mouth.

Your body doesn't know why you are smiling or carrying yourself like a prize fighter about to go twelve rounds; it just senses you are and responds appropriately. You might feel funny ducking into a bathroom before a big meeting so that you can lift your hands high for a couple minutes while you say a prayer and think through what you are going to say. But it's a whole lot better than sitting at your desk wringing your hands. When the stress melts away into confidence, you'll be glad you did.

I hear your objections: *I can't show that kind of zeal if it isn't how I feel, because that wouldn't be real.* Let me warn you that this kind of thinking is why so many marriages fall apart and why so many people never experience the breakthroughs God has for them. People who do the right things only when they feel them never enter into the victorious life. Worship is not a feeling expressed through actions; it's an act of obedience that, once expressed, often leads to feelings. Simply put, you do it because it is right. And in God's grace, many times the emotions follow suit.

I will never speak without going through an important ritual. I kneel in prayer and admit my weaknesses so that I can enter into Christ's strength. You can't rise like a lion if you don't first kneel like a lamb. There are also very specific prayers that I pray and words that I speak over myself.

In the last moment before taking the stage, I always say the following:

I am a son of the king.

I have the spirit that raised Christ from the dead.

I can do all things through Christ who gives me strength.

I am as bold as a lion.

Forcing these words to come out of my mouth, whether I feel them in the moment or not, causes me to step into what is true about me. It puts me into the frame of mind in which I am not trying to impress people but am sent by God to bless people, a mind-set in which I'm seeking to give a gift, not to receive one. This stops me from looking for validation by reminding me I am already valued. You don't need to earn what you already have. Rooting my identity gives me strength for that day's activity.

If all this preparation seems like overkill, realize that the benefit of purposely heightening the intensity before the game begins is decreased pressure once it does. Remember Alan Shepard? One fascinating thing he said about that inaugural flight was how anticlimactic it was. Everyone had worked so hard to prepare him for the rigors of the launch—he completed 120 test flights—they had unintentionally *over*prepared him.

YOU CAN'T
RISE
— LIKE A —
LION
IF YOU DON'T
FIRST
KNEEL
— LIKE A —
LAMB

He kept waiting for it to get crazy, but it was underwhelming in comparison to what he had done in preparation. Engineers had put more G-force generating capability into the centrifuge he trained on than the rocket actually generated. The speakers they put next to his head with recordings of rocket engines were much louder than what he experienced being locked in a sealed capsule that muffled the sounds outside. He said his cooling fan was one of the loudest noises he heard.

We're tempted to phone it in while merely practicing and really turn it on when it is game time: *I'll work hard to prepare a message when the Bible study is not just for a small youth group. I'll memorize the songs instead of reading off a music stand when I lead worship at a bigger church. I'll hustle when I get promoted and have more responsibility. I'll write if and when I get a book deal.*

What Shepard discovered was that the more stress applied to your training, the less you'll stress when it is time to shine. Public victory comes from private discipline. If you aren't busting your butt to kill it where you are, God isn't going to turn up the volume on your life. He isn't going to export to greater platforms what isn't working at home.

When my editor read this chapter, she told me about Tessa Virtue and Scott Moir, two Olympic ice dancers who always embrace before they perform so they can match their breathing and heartbeats and build their connection to each other. That is beautiful. And it is for that same reason you shouldn't just rush to class or work without spending a few moments speaking to and listening to God. That "hug" allows you to match your heart to his.

No matter what is in front of you today—be it a stadium

full of people you're performing in front of, a rocket launch taking you to Mars, a classroom of students you're speaking to, or a toddler you're parenting—this much is true: you're not ready to face the game until you put your game face on.

PHANTOM POWER

WHAT YOU HAVE

THE HELP YOU NEED TO WIN THIS WAR

NEVER BRING A HORSE
TO A TANK FIGHT

*You shall receive power when the Holy Spirit
has come upon you; and you shall be witnesses
to Me in Jerusalem, and in all Judea and
Samaria, and to the end of the earth.*

—Jesus

I stand by everything I've given you in the three cards we've laid on the table. But without the fourth card, all I have done is saddled you up on a horse and sent you off to fight a tank all by yourself. That isn't winning the war—it's committing suicide.

Positive thinking is important; so is watching how you speak and minding your habits. But if that is all you walk away with, then this book is simply self-help. There is something much better than self-help—God's help. Without it, all the self-management strategies and the tips for growing your emotional intelligence will leave you powerless when it comes to true and lasting change.

As I said, riding out to do battle against a tank on horseback seems like a really bad idea. But in the incredible but true story depicted in the movie *12 Strong*, that's exactly what happened. *12 Strong* takes place in the days after 9/11, when al-Qaeda hunkered down in the mountains of Afghanistan. An unbelievably brave contingent of soldiers, led by a character played by Chris Hemsworth, agreed to join forces with a local warlord who promised to get them within striking distance of the terrorists. The only problem was that they didn't know for sure if they could trust the warlord; there were prices on their heads from the moment they set foot in the country, and allegiances shifted every day. Oh, and they would have to travel via horseback, as there was no way to sneak up on al-Qaeda using traditional vehicles in the mountain passes.

The most jaw-dropping scene takes place when the soldiers charge onto the battlefield up against machine-gun-laden pickup trucks and even full-blown tanks. The Americans had only the guns and grenades they carried with them. They would have been doomed if that were the end of the story, but they also had a laser pointer and a satellite phone. With those two vital pieces of equipment they were able to call for fire to rain from the sky. It wasn't what they brought into the battle that made them dangerous but rather who was on the other end of the phone—namely the most powerful military in the history of mankind. B-52 bombers circled overhead; all the soldiers had to do was mark the target with the laser and give the command on their phone. Remember, he who controls the high ground controls the outcome.

Early in the book I referenced Paul's fit of despair in which he bemoaned his inability to help himself. Remember how he said it? "I am not practicing what I would like to do, but I am doing the very thing I hate" (Romans 7:15 NASB).

If it were possible to do better on our own, we wouldn't need God. We would simply follow the golden rule, and all would be fine. The problem is that we are fallen and bent towards sinful choices. There are none who seek God; no, not one (Romans 3:10–12). If this weren't the case, God never would have sent his Son to die for us; instead, he could have just told us to be good. As a matter of fact, that was what the whole Moses on Mt. Sinai thing was about. The Ten Commandments were essentially God telling us to help ourselves. It didn't even last ten minutes, and then there was a drunken orgy and a golden calf followed by complete and total anarchy.

Paul didn't finish his outburst by saying, "I guess I'll just try harder . . ." Instead he said, "Thanks be to God through Jesus Christ our Lord!" (Romans 7:25 NASB). Relying on Jesus is our secret weapon, the ace of spades that no card can beat.

The message of the gospel isn't *try*; it's *trust*. It's what puts you in contact with power from on high. You want to talk about air superiority? There is nothing so high as the most high. God, who dwells in heaven and waits to send his ultimate power in response to your asking in faith and receiving it with a mind to act on it. This doesn't make the other things we have talked about irrelevant; it makes them supremely significant. Being energized by God is like plugging into a power source. There's a night-and-day difference between using a coffee machine or

THE MESSAGE
OF THE
GOSPEL

ISN'T TRY
IT'S
TRUST

---

a curling iron that is plugged in versus using one that is just sitting on the counter.

One. Two. We!

There seems to be a divide between those who say that God helps those who help themselves and those who insist God helps those who *can't* help themselves. I think they are two sides of the same coin.

It is true that salvation is all about grace. We are dead in sin, and dead people can't rise—no matter what they do. On the other hand, once Jesus has raised us from the dead, he expects us to apply ourselves effectively, working out what he has worked in us. You should pray like it is all up to God and work like it is all up to you. Or to put it in financial vernacular: think like a millionaire but hustle like you're broke.

You see a picture of this when Jesus raised a little girl from the dead (Mark 5:35–43). Her resurrection was all Jesus. She added nothing to it. That is us without God—hopeless, lost, and completely unable to change our state. But once she came back to life, Jesus told her family to give her something to eat (v. 43). Why did he raise her from the dead but insist that they be the ones to feed her? God will never do for us what we can do for ourselves.

We see the same thing when Jesus raised Lazarus from the dead. Jesus was the one who caused Lazarus's coagulated blood to flow through his dried-up veins, but then he told those there to unwrap him from the grave clothes. It is God alone who can give the miraculous, but he expects you to live out of and take care of your miracles.

We are not to wage war according to our own resources. The power that leads to victory is not in us or from us; it is with God and comes to us from his hand. But that same power has to be wielded. Having it and using it are two completely different things. My brother bought me a Movie Pass card that allows me to see a movie in the theater every twenty-four hours. It sits there in my wallet whether I see any movies or not. The same is true of gym memberships; just because you have the right to go to the gym and freely utilize the equipment doesn't automatically mean you get a six-pack. You have to walk in and take advantage of what your membership gives you access to.

So it is when it comes to the arsenal of power at your beck and call as a child of God. Peter wrote, "His divine power has given to us all things that pertain to life and godliness, through the knowledge of Him who called us by glory and virtue" (2 Peter 1:3). Do you have all things that pertain to life and godliness? Potentially you do, but practically you have to tap into what belongs to you, one moment at a time.

Paul made a similar statement: "Blessed be the God and Father of our Lord Jesus Christ, who has blessed us with every spiritual blessing in the heavenly places in Christ" (Ephesians 1:3). Are you thinking, *Wait a minute, I have "every spiritual blessing in the heavenly places in Christ"? Where are all these blessings?* They are at the same place the biceps and abs you wish you had are—waiting for you to take advantage of. They won't work if you won't work them.

How pitiful it would have been for the Americans to try to duke it out on their own instead of calling on the B-52 bombers that were waiting for them! That's what we do when we try to fight spiritual battles using only human strategies.

Keep that picture in mind as you read these words from 2 Corinthians 10: "For though we walk in the flesh, we do not wage war according to the flesh. For the weapons of our warfare are not carnal but mighty in God for pulling down strongholds, casting down arguments and every high thing that exalts itself against the knowledge of God, bringing every thought into captivity to the obedience of Christ" (vv. 3–5).

One of the biggest mistakes you can make is to try to do God's work without God's power. There's a great scene in *Iron Man 3* where Tony Stark's autopilot malfunctions, and he flies hundreds of miles out of the way, crash landing in snow-covered Rose Hill, Tennessee. Feeling claustrophobic, he ejects. But then once he realizes how "brisk" it is in the snow, he wishes he had stayed in the coziness of the suit.

He trudges through the snow, carrying the Iron Man suit behind him like a kid pulling a sled. He is totally huffing and puffing as he slowly pulls it one foot at a time. It's a perfect visual because the suit wasn't designed to be carried *by* him; it was designed to carry him as he executed his calling as a superhero.

The Bible says that we are *in* Christ. "In Christ" is a theological term to describe the way God sees us as being completely covered in Jesus. But when it comes to fighting battles, you can also think of being in Christ the way Tony is in the Iron Man suit. Through our continued reliance on Jesus, we tap into an arsenal of protection, ammunition, and navigation.

So many Christians are struggling to pull what should propel them, trying to fight the battles of this life with their own strength, waging war according to the flesh. Don't make that error! Stay in the suit. Jesus is not something to carry like a religious trinket or good-luck charm, He is a risen Lord who will carry you. Call for firepower, and when God makes the ground shake with energy, be ready to occupy the territory he has cleared with the commonsense strategies of the first three cards. You have to maintain what he gives you the power to obtain.

But what about the strongholds Paul mentioned that we need God's power to take down? Most ancient cities had a fortress, a stronghold, on top of a hill in which its residents could take refuge. The Corinthians would have been tracking with him as he used this language, because high above the ancient city of Corinth was a 1,883-foot-tall hill upon which stood a fortress. If you controlled that fortress, you controlled the city.

In chapter 2 we learned the importance of possessing the high ground. A stronghold provides many benefits. For one, you can see the enemy coming so it's harder to be taken by surprise. For another, you have light on your side, because the enemy has to look up into the sun to see you. When someone else has an elevated position over you, you are a sitting duck, an easy target.

In your life, a stronghold is an area in which you have become entrenched in believing something that isn't true, or in doing something you shouldn't be doing, and as a result the enemy has a heavily fortified position in your life. Simply put: it's a constant pull in the wrong direction.

These strongholds can take many forms: pride, anxiety, lust, resentment, jealousy, bitterness, condemnation, shame, physical abuse, substance abuse, addictions, jealousy and covetousness, eating disorders, compulsive behavior, low self-esteem—the list goes on and on.

STRONGHOLDS ARE A CONSTANT PULL IN THE WRONG DIRECTION

These strongholds put a chokehold on the joy, growth, free-dom, and strength you are meant to experience. They neutralize your effectiveness and lock you in a state of arrested develop-ment. This much is for sure—you'll never experience all that life holds if you're living with strongholds. They're like having a blockage in your arteries. No matter how hard your heart pumps, you just can't get necessary blood flow to your body.

It is worth noting that you don't have to demolish a strong-hold that was never built in the first place. That is why you should be exceedingly cautious about what you allow into your life. If we spend more energy on prevention, we wouldn't need to spend nearly as much time on cure. I would rather wash my hands, get rest, stay hydrated, and get a flu shot than spend a ton of money on NyQuil and Theraflu, zinc, colloidal silver, and apple cider vinegar.

It's the same with your soul. An ounce of prevention is worth a pound of cure. It's such a bad idea to toy with sin, because footholds turn into strongholds. A little leaven leavens the whole loaf (Galatians 5:9). The biggest mistake you can make is to underestimate your enemy—he's playing chess, not checkers, and wants to get a beachhead in your life.

You might be making a relatively small compromise here or there—like dating someone you shouldn't, or watching raun-chy movies and thinking, *I can handle this*. Maybe you can, but he's looking for anything to get you to justify something.

We shouldn't allow small things to add up, but what if we already have? Our God is able! Yes, an ounce of prevention is worth a pound of cure, but the good news is God has a pound of cure too! It is never too late to do the right thing.

Are there things that have a really strong hold on you?

Things that are constantly pulling you in the wrong direction? Here's how to demolish them:

1. Spot them. Ask God to open your eyes to hidden sins so you can identify them and recognize them for what they are—areas of oppression in which sin has barricaded itself and the enemy has a power position against you. We are all blind to our own blind spots.
2. Renounce the thinking or behavior and set your soul against it. This is called *repentance*.
3. Paint the target so heaven can blast it with God's supernatural power.
4. Let your squad in on what has been going on. God alone can forgive, but other people are needed to walk in healing (James 5:16).
5. Vigilantly and diligently build something in place of the sin so it can never be rebuilt. If you don't follow up your new start with a new plan, the stronghold will be taken again, and it will be seven times worse than the first time. Getting triple-bypass heart surgery is only effective if the patient exercises and follows a low-cholesterol diet afterward. Otherwise he ends up right where he was before the surgery.

Let me expand on the third step—paint the target. Hold the laser on the stronghold so that when you give the code word, the bombers know where to drop their payload. To do this effectively you need to use precise language. Every mission has a clear code word used to authenticate the command. In *Black Hawk Down*, for example, the word was *Irene*.

We, too, have been given a word, and it is a name. Philippians 2:10 says, *"At the name of Jesus* every knee should bow, of those in heaven, and of those on earth, and of those under the earth."

You can force your enemies to their knees by being willing to kneel on yours. As the old hymn put it, "Satan trembles, when he sees the weakest saint upon his knees." Prayer is a weapon that turns off darkness. And as you pray, make sure you use the right word. The name of Jesus—not just a generic *God* or *the man upstairs*—is what gives us power.

I heard recently that the TV show *MythBusters* was originally called *Tall Tales or True*, but the show was rejected when it was pitched to the Discovery Channel. It wasn't until it got the name *MythBusters* that it was given the green light.

Words matter. God has given us a name that is above every name, and his appointed power floods in when we use it. Omitting it is a huge mistake.

Discover what David said is possible when you are willing to call in God's help as you declare war on all that holds you back:

> He trains my hands for battle;
>> my arms can bend a bow of bronze.
> You make your saving help my shield,
>> and your right hand sustains me;
>> your help has made me great.
> You provide a broad path for my feet,
>> so that my ankles do not give way.
>
> I pursued my enemies and overtook them;
>> I did not turn back till they were destroyed.

I crushed them so that they could not rise;
> they fell beneath my feet.
You armed me with strength for battle;
> you humbled my adversaries before me.
You made my enemies turn their backs in flight,
> and I destroyed my foes.
They cried for help, but there was no one to save them—
> to the LORD, but he did not answer.
I beat them as fine as windblown dust;
> I trampled them like mud in the streets.
You have delivered me from the attacks of the people;
> you have made me the head of nations.
People I did not know now serve me,
> foreigners cower before me;
> as soon as they hear of me, they obey me.
They all lose heart;
> they come trembling from their strongholds. (Psalm 18:34–45 NIV)

David knew what he was talking about. As a young man he had walked into the valley of Elah to uproot a giant named Goliath who had been blaspheming God for forty days. Everyone in Israel cowered in response to this great enemy who was entrenched in his superiority over them. David was a lot like a horseback rider going up against a tank as he walked up to fight this man of war with only a slingshot and a shepherd's staff. It seemed he was outgunned in every way. Goliath roared in rage, saliva flying from his grotesque lips as he promised to paint the ground red with David's blood. But David didn't trust in the weapons in his hands; he painted Goliath red by invoking "the name of the LORD of hosts, the God of the armies of Israel" (1 Samuel 17:45).

When you fight your battles in the name of Jesus, your enemies won't have any more power over you than the giant did over David that day in the Valley of Elah. As Goliath's corpse hit the earth, and the dust settled, it was evident that even with his 125-pound coat of armor, enormous javelin, spear, and helmet, Goliath was the one who brought the horse to the tank fight.

BUTTERFLIES AND EAGLES

Mistakes aren't a necessary evil. They aren't evil at all. They are an inevitable consequence of doing something new (and, as such, should be seen as valuable).

—ED CATMULL

Have you ever said under your breath, *This is too hard; it's more than I can bear*? If so, you're right. You can't.

It always happened at recess, and it always involved falling—off a slide, off the swings, off a fence. I guess I just fell a lot as a kid. Seconds seemed like hours as I'd try to get my lungs to expand. I was sure I was going to die. This would continue for what seemed like an eternity, until all of a sudden everything would be okay—and then I'd immediately go back to playing, like nothing happened.

What I didn't know then was that there is more than one way to get the wind knocked out of you.

I found the limits of what my breath could do when I tried to give my daughter Lenya CPR in the final moments of her life on earth. My breath in her lungs wasn't enough to sustain her, and despite my best efforts, she died and went to heaven, leaving us here with the wind knocked out of us. Five years have passed, and in that time the concussive power of that devastating explosion has sent ripples through our home that have caused us to lose our breath time after time—often when we least expect it. *This is more than we can bear* has crossed my mind more times than I can count.

If you haven't yet faced anything so hard it pushed you to the absolute breaking point, your day will come. I don't mean that disrespectfully; it's just a fact. If you live long enough to love deeply, you will hurt significantly. Everyone has a breaking point, no matter how gallant or brave or strong. Even the very thing keeping you alive—your breath—is limited.

It's been said that time makes fools of us all. I'd like to amend that—time makes *frail beings* of us all. Even the youth grow weary, and the strong man fails. Everyone you and I know and care about will eventually get sick, wounded, or injured; eventually we all die. To be devastated is the door prize of being mortal.

That's why it is so important that you don't try to fight these battles in your own strength or by relying on your own lung power. When your breath is taken away, you need to rely on God for a second wind. The first wind is your natural air given to you at creation, when God breathed into the dust he formed us out of. The second wind is the power of the Holy Spirit given to us after Jesus rose from the dead.

The disciples were gathered in the Upper Room when Jesus

appeared in their midst and proved he was alive by allowing them to touch his body. Then he did the same thing he did in the garden of Eden: he gave them air. "He breathed on them, and said to them, 'Receive the Holy Spirit'" (John 20:22).

I understand if your antenna shoots up when I bring up the Holy Spirit. But stay with me; this isn't cultish or denominational—it's scriptural. This is an area in which there has been plenty of abuse, but neglect is abuse too. And neglecting the Holy Spirit is like declining the offer of a friend with a truck to help you move, and instead opting to drag your furniture by yourself down the road.

The Holy Spirit is the secret to victorious living. He wants to turbocharge your efforts to live for God and help you prevail in the war with the version of you that you don't want to be. All you have to do is ask God to give you strength, and he will come upon you like a mighty rushing wind, propelling you to places you could never go otherwise. This is the key to being the mom you always wanted to be, handling conflict with your father as you wish you could, being a real-estate agent who is great at your job, and bravely going through chemotherapy like a bright, shining light. I want you to know about his strength so that you don't quit thinking right, speaking right, and doing right.

In the Old Testament, the priests who served in the temple had to go through a process before they could report for duty. There were cleansing rituals with water and a ceremony that involved getting dressed. But before they could punch in, they were to be anointed with blood and then oil. Blood was the symbol of forgiveness, and it was dabbed on the ear, the thumb, and the big toe. Its purpose was to cleanse you from where you walked, what you heard, and what you handled. The priests understood the oil to be a symbol of being set apart, but now that we have the full revelation of God's Word, we know that oil was symbolic of the anointing of the Holy Spirit. Today, through Christ, we are kings and priests, "a chosen people, a royal priesthood, a holy nation, God's special possession" (1 Peter 2:9 NIV).

We don't need just the forgiveness that comes at salvation; we need help, power from on high. Today too many believers are saved, but do not enjoy the empowerment. We need the blood and the oil, the cross and the comforter.

The prolific preacher Charles Spurgeon wrote,

> If there were only one prayer which I might pray before I died, it should be this: Lord, send to Your Church men filled with the Holy Spirit, and with fire.
>
> The church is weak today because the Holy Spirit is not upon her members as we could desire him to be. You and I are tottering along like feeble babes, whereas, had we more of the Spirit, we might walk without fainting, run without weariness, and even mount up with wings as eagles.

So many Jesus followers have come through Calvary but neglected Pentecost. The result is they end up as spiritual butterflies instead of soaring eagles. Jesus promised to put his power in our lungs. But if we don't ask for that power, we are forgiven but not fueled for service. We flutter along, blown off course by the smallest breeze, when we are meant to cut through the air majestically and full of strength.

It has been said that if the Holy Spirit were withdrawn

from the church today, 95 percent of what we do would go on, and no one would know the difference. This is a travesty! We should be so reliant on the Holy Ghost that were he to leave we would instantly feel like an astronaut without an oxygen supply.

Two Steps to the Left

There's a walking path that I frequent when I'm studying and I hit a brain block. Over the years I have had some seriously impressive times on it with the Lord. I find I pray better walking, I think better walking. It's just rejuvenating to my spirit. I'll grab my dog, Tabasco, throw a slip of paper and a pen in my pocket, and, most importantly, leave my phone on the kitchen counter.

When my daughter Lenya went home to heaven, one of the most important ways I coped was through walking this path and telling God exactly how I was feeling. I have written more sermon points and come up with more ideas for messages on this path than I have probably anywhere else in the world.

I am usually not completely there, just walking and thinking and praying and sometimes singing. People I encounter probably assume I'm crazy, as I'm usually muttering or writing something on a slip of paper balanced on my thigh.

A few months back on one of these walks, I snapped back to reality and noticed I was walking in a strange fashion, almost like I was playing hopscotch or walking on a bridge with random planks out. I realized I was being careful to avoid all the little gifts that had been left on the path by a flock of

Canada geese that live in the area during the warmer months of the year. It's normal for them to leave droppings here and there, but on this particular day it was ridiculous. The path was covered with poop. At a certain point there was almost no exposed pavement. I don't know what kind of deranged party they were having, but if any Canada geese are reading, I do not want an invitation.

Yet I persisted. I have a certain point in the path where I turn around, and to not get to that point would send me into an OCD frenzy. I needed to get there, so I kept going.

Let it never be said that a Canada goose ever got the best of me. I almost had to do the splits with each step, like Will Ferrell going up the escalator in *Elf*. I finally got to the end of the path and turned around only to realize, *I've got to do this all over again.* I was disgusted, plus I already nearly had a charley horse.

As I began to take careful steps, I looked to my left and noticed a green, grassy belt running parallel to the path. Apparently it had not been pleasing to these geese as they were relieving themselves. It was completely clean, completely open. I felt pretty stupid as I realized that the entire time I had been walking through the landmines, I could have been walking on the grass. I took two steps to my left, and from then on it was smooth sailing all the way home.

I think that illustrates the difference between trying to live for God and letting God's life live through you. It was a tiny change—just two steps to the left—and I went from moving like an awkward butterfly to moving like an eagle.

It might not be that you need a huge change to achieve significant forward progress. You might be moving in the right direction, just making it harder on yourself than you need to. You might have been walking a path strewn with what the apostle Paul said he learned to count as dung—human achievement (Philippians 3:8). Once he learned to rely on the Spirit's power, he still gave just as much effort, perhaps even more. God's grace never makes you want to do less; instead you are open to going above and beyond, because you know it's no longer about you.

Perhaps the shift from self-power to Spirit power will be like taking two steps to your left and going the same direction you were before but now seeing God dramatically bless your efforts.

That's the message God gave to Zerubbabel in the Old Testament book of Zechariah. (If you don't know where that is here's a pro-tip: find Matthew, the first book of the New Testament, and go two steps to the left.) With permission from Cyrus the king, Zerubbabel brought 42,360 of his closest friends with him to Jerusalem. Zerubbabel's goal was to build the temple that had been torn down during the Babylonian invasion in 586 BC when Nebuchadnezzar overtook Judah and brought them to Babylon in chains to live as captives.

God called Zerubbabel to rebuild the house of God. It was dangerous and risky and difficult, especially without walls to protect them. When they asked God how they could possibly be safe without walls protecting them from invasion, God told them, "I will protect you, not with walls of wood and stone but with a wall of fire!" (Zechariah 2:5, author's paraphrase).

What a comforting thought! I have a security system and a gun and a baseball bat to keep my kids safe. I love that my

GOD'S GRACE
NEVER
MAKES YOU WANT
TO DO
LESS
BECAUSE YOU
★ KNOW ★
IT'S NO
LONGER
ABOUT YOU

next-door neighbor is a police officer, and I have three other cops on my speed dial. But the greatest comfort is knowing that God keeps my home surrounded with walls of flame!

That was enough for Zerubbabel, so he and his crew got to work. They worked for almost nine years, but after nearly a decade of labor they still had almost no progress to show for it. They were met with opposition, barriers, discouragement, and unforeseen problems. And of course there were fights and division, because let's face it—you can't accomplish anything great without criticism and hardship. Every day they were trying and trying and trying, and it was just not working, not working, not working.

It makes you feel for Zerubbabel. It's hard enough to keep a team motivated and on track and fired up when you can point to visible success. "See what's happening? Look what we got to do. How many of you know we're going to do more of this?" But for nine years, he was trying to help people believe in the dream when they had no progress to be encouraged by.

Zerubbabel would have felt discouraged and tired. His wheels were spinning in the mud, and he couldn't get any traction. This is when doubts creep in: *Maybe I'm not the guy. Maybe I'm not cut out for this. Maybe we should leave it to someone else.*

He fell into an emotional funk, but God spoke to and quickened his heart and, through an angel, gave Zechariah a vision for Zerubbabel. Zechariah saw a golden lampstand— interestingly enough, the same kind of lampstand that would be in the temple in Jerusalem, if they ever finished it. In the vision the work on the temple was completely done, and this was a lampstand like no one had ever seen before.

This big, elaborate golden lampstand had seven flames on it, and above it was an enormous golden bowl. The bowl was situated just below two enormous olive trees that were producing olives. As soon as an olive would ripen, it would drop off the tree into the waiting bowl beneath.

The olives would be pressed into olive oil, which would run into seven tubes attached to the bottom of the bowl. Each of the tubes went to one of the flames of fire. Unlike the torch in the temple, which required oil to be added daily, this was a never-ending supply that fueled a never-ending flame. It was an eternal fire—perpetually burning and completely self-sustaining.

The vision came with the following instructions:

"This is the word of the LORD to Zerubbabel:
'Not by might nor by power, but by My Spirit,'
Says the Lord of hosts." (Zechariah 4:6)

Game changer. This was the missing piece: secret power. Zerubbabel was going to be doing the same thing he had been doing before, but now he would be relying on God's strength instead of his own. A tiny tweak would create an enormous difference, because he wouldn't be trying to soldier through or grit it out to make it happen. Instead, he was going to take two steps to the left and get into the lane called *grace*. By relying on God's strength, he would be able to fulfill God's call. Trusting in the Holy Spirit, Zechariah and the people did the impossible—mountains were made plains before them, and the final stone was put in place with shouts of "Grace! Grace!" (Zechariah 4:7).

Is This Thing On?

Perhaps the word of God to Zerubbabel is the word of God to you too. Are you at your wit's end in your marriage? On your last nerve with your kids? Running on empty at work? Maybe you are trying to do the right thing but are relying on your own power. It doesn't matter how many times a butterfly flaps its wings; it cannot soar where an eagle can, because eagles can ride on winds butterfly wings can't tap into. Imagine what a huge difference it would make in your life to have the power of the Holy Ghost's wind in your sails.

The disciples could never have taken the gospel to the ends of the earth and turned the Roman empire upside down without the Holy Spirit's empowering them; that's why they were to wait until they received power from on high. It is no different for you. There are amazing, remarkable things God wants to do on your college campus, at your place of business, and in your neighborhood. But first you need to ask Jesus to breathe on you and give you his strength. And you will need to do it again tomorrow, because power is perishable. The minutes don't roll over.

Audio technicians deal with something called *phantom power*—the ability to send power to certain devices from the soundboard. Certain types of microphones require phantom power in order to function. The phantom power must be specifically turned on for that channel if you want to hear your voice.

Ephesians 4:7 tells us about God's phantom power: "To each one of us grace was given according to the measure of Christ's gift." God, the master soundman, will never hand you a gift and call you to do something without also being willing to give you the elecricity to power the gift. Bottom line: you can't win the war within without asking God every day to energize your efforts and then being sensitive to the cues he gives you along the way. Like the rumble strip on the side of the highway, God directs us through gentle nudges to correct our courses.

No matter what God calls you to do, his command comes with enablement. The air force doesn't expect you to bring your own F-16; they give you all you need to fulfill your orders. You also don't need to understand how you're going to complete your mission. You just need to say okay and then obey. There will always be a million reasons to hesitate:

- *It's not a good time to tithe right now.*
- *It's not practical for us to move out right now—I know we're not married, but surely God understands.*
- *I'll start that business or go back to school one of these days. I just don't see how it could happen in this economy.*
- *I would share the gospel with my neighbor if he brought up a spiritual topic, but all he ever talks about is sports.*

It will never be convenient to obey. But when you do what God has said, you'll experience power and blessing and peace.

Decide to obey God and then let him work out the details. "Trust in the LORD with all your heart, and lean not on your own understanding; in all your ways acknowledge Him, and He shall direct your paths" (Proverbs 3:5–6). The end result will be that you see him magnificently work things out, but first you have to take the gutsy step of faith that says, *I believe.*

GOD
DIRECTS
— US —
THROUGH
GENTLE
NUDGES
* TO CORRECT *
OUR
COURSES

He's got the power; you just need to ask for it. He is a good Father. He won't give you a tarantula if you ask for a Fruit Roll-Up. But he will give you the Holy Spirit if you ask him to.

Try it. And when you get the wind knocked out of you, ask for a second wind, and a third, and a fourth. If you're knocked down seven times, he'll give you a seventh wind too.

A TRIP TO THE DUMP

Revivals don't last and neither do baths.

—ATTRIBUTED TO BILLY SUNDAY

I have an idea for Amazon. They should work out a deal with UPS where they take an empty box *away* from your house whenever they deliver a package *to* your house. It can be recycled or reused or turned into gerbil food or whatever. Most importantly, they'd be ridding my garage of boxes.

It is really a problem. Or maybe *I* have a problem, but I am offering the world a solution. I just hope someone high-up at Amazon is reading this.

I'd like to say I have this issue only around the holidays, but that wouldn't be telling the truth. It is just a huge issue, period. You can buy everything online with one-click conveni-ence. The situation came to a head a couple months ago when I couldn't get to where I keep my tools to grab a screwdriver. I'm not saying it was hard to get to my tools or that I had to move some stuff around—I physically couldn't walk into the garage because the boxes had taken over the world.

At the beginning of the year, we challenged our entire church to do a seven-day fast so we could recenter our hearts on heaven. I decided to take the week off from not just food but from buying anything online or even researching things to buy online (reading reviews, watching YouTube videos, and so on). I wouldn't visit any e-commerce site or app of any kind, read blogs, or visit fashion websites describing new trends or styles.

It was honestly more challenging for me than giving up food! I found myself constantly thinking of things I needed to buy. Little stuff like toothpaste and a new propeller blade to replace the one that broke on my drone. It was eye-opening how often my reflex in a slow moment was to go shop online.

One day toward the end of the week, when we were sitting down to family dinner, we saw the UPS truck go by our house. Clover, my youngest daughter, blurted out, "The UPS truck didn't stop at our house!" And her older sister Daisy exclaimed, "That's never happened before!"

I finally decided to do something about it the day I could no longer get into the garage. Our normal strategy is to cut up a few boxes at a time so that they fit in our trash can. But the flow of boxes coming in was far exceeding our ability to get them out, and every passing week we were getting further behind. So I put an audiobook on in my headphones, grabbed a box cutter, and went to work cutting down the army of boxes. Then I filled up every square inch of my SUV and took them to the giant cardboard recycling receptacle at the dump. It took two full trips. (You know you have a problem when . . .) It felt so good to have the garage purified of the evidence of the overuse of our Prime membership. Afterward I paraded my entire family around the garage, exclaiming how happy I was to have our lives back.

A couple of weeks later, I was shocked to see the boxes already piling up again. I threw on a Patagonia fleece, cranked up another audiobook, and got busy. Since then it has become an every-other-Sunday ritual for me. After church I eat lunch, crash for forty-five minutes, and then gear up for my biweekly trip to the garbage dump.

I don't know why, but I find it to be cathartic. There's just something so satisfying about getting rid of garbage. It makes me feel like a new person. Driving away without the pile of boxes I feel lighter, happier, and more satisfied. And I do this on a Sunday, I also feel like symbolically it represents how all the pressures and the expectations of the previous week are now over, giving way to the new week. The purge hits reset on my mind.

The truth is that we all need to undergo a similar kind of purge on the inside. We accumulate gunk and grime and shame in our hearts and minds, and we need an outlet for all that junk. This is why confession is such an important part of our relationship with God. First John 1:9 says, "But if we confess our sins to him, he is faithful and just to forgive us our sins and to cleanse us from all wickedness" (NLT). As we sin and are hurt and get offended and offend others, the garages of our hearts get filled with trash and boxes and hurt feelings and regrets. If we don't have a place to take those things, they pile up and cause us harm. Just as our phones and computers get sluggish and freeze up when they are overcrowded, so our souls can't receive the new files God wants us to download when it has been too long since old things were wiped away.

It is interesting to me that even when people don't believe in God, they still look for an outlet for the negative thoughts and emotions that accumulate. I recently stayed in a hotel in downtown Portland that had a landing with a view overlooking the lobby. Decorated with couches and tables, it was a great place to drink coffee while you worked on your laptop or caught up with a friend. Randomly scattered about the room were freshly sharpened #2 pencils with the hotel logo on them and little pads of paper. Against one wall was an enormous, antique-looking wooden cabinet. Covered with small drawers, it looked like it had at one point been used to store library catalog cards.

(Hold that thought. The doorbell just rang; it was UPS delivering a package from Amazon full of Nespresso capsules. You can't make this stuff up.)

Anyway, I opened up one of the drawers, and tucked inside were dozens and dozens of the little papers from the pads of papers on the tables. They were unsigned, anonymous notes written by people who had stopped in at the hotel. Some of them were poems or thoughts or notes, but it seemed that most of them contained secrets that people wanted to get off their chests—things they had either done or had wanted to do. A few were pretty terrible. Some were petty. Some of them made me very, very sad. And even though it was a little creepy, I could have stayed there for hours reading them.

I thought of that wooden chest of drawers when I was making my most recent voyage to purge the cardboard. The same reason it feels good for me to rid the garage of boxes is probably what makes those people unburden their souls to a piece of furniture at a hotel. The only difference between scribbling a note on a piece of paper and bringing your trials and transgressions to God in prayer is that he has the power to forgive you and scrub you clean with a power washer.

Confessing your sin to God is a trip to the dump for your soul. Imagine if you had no way to take the garbage out of your home for a month. What would it smell like? How unpleasant would it be to live surrounded by spoiled food, broken appliances, empty wrappers, used Q-tips, and dirty, threadbare underwear?

In 2013 all six thousand garbage collectors in Madrid, Spain, went on strike. After only eight days the city was overrun with trash, and the streets were "brimming with garbage, including litter, rotting food and dog excrement." People were soon at a breaking point begging for the trash collectors to return.

Here's the point: what's true of a home and a city is also true in your head and in your heart. Without a regular purge, your soul will quickly become overrun with the stinking thinking and rotting feelings that accumulate over time. Whenever I let my guard down and let Evilevi take the wheel he leaves garbage everywhere that needs somewhere to go. By bringing crummy feelings to God the moment I spot them it keeps my alter-ego from rearing his head in the first place. If you are going to function at the level God wants you to, taking out the emotional and spiritual trash needs to become a daily part of your life. The Holy Spirit is the one who shows you what things need to go and takes them away when you confess them.

WITHOUT A REGULAR PURGE YOUR SOUL

WILL QUICKLY ★ BECOME ★ OVERRUN WITH STINKING THINKING —AND— ROTTING FEELINGS

The Importance of Spot Cleaning

This spiritual trip to the dump is what Jesus had in mind during the Last Supper when he washed the disciples' feet. The disciples had been arguing about who was the greatest, and right there, right then, Jesus modeled true greatness for them by stooping to serve them. He taught them what real leadership is all about—serving people.

Peter objected, saying that he would never let Jesus touch his feet. Jesus responded, "If I do not wash you, you have no part with Me" (John 13:8).

Peter relented and said, "Lord, not my feet only, but also my hands and my head!" (v. 9). Never one to do something halfway, Peter went from being unwilling to have his feet cleaned to wanting an entire full-body sponge bath!

Jesus politely declined and said, "He who is bathed needs only to wash his feet, but is completely clean" (v. 10).

Initially, this verse was quite confusing to me. I'm sure that there are a lot of seven-year-old boys who would use it as an excuse at bath time: "Jesus said I don't need a bath—I just need to wash my feet!" It becomes clearer when you understand that there are two very different words for "wash" being used here—one indicates the whole body being cleaned in a bath, head to toe. The other describes a spot cleaning—where after a thorough washing you would clean the part of the body that had become dirty.

In that day, it was customary to take a bath and get all cleaned up before going to someone's house or to a feast. But because people wore sandals, when they walked down the dirt roads, their feet would get dirty. When they arrived, they would be clean except for their feet. Only their feet would need to be washed to restore them to a fully clean state.

On a spiritual level Jesus is describing two distinct washings—one done once, to become thoroughly clean, the other done as needed on an ongoing basis. The first washing takes place when you become a Christian. Titus 3:5 says, "Not by works of righteousness which we have done, but according to His mercy He saved us, through the washing of regeneration and renewing of the Holy Spirit."

Salvation is more powerful than any cleaner on the market today. Better than Tide, OxiClean, Comet, Scrubbing Bubbles, or even bleach. Jesus washes us clean from our sins with his blood—the only cleaning agent that can do the job, so effective it only needs to be done once.

The second washing is a spot cleaning to take care of the daily things that get on us, that come from walking in a dirty, wicked world. Our hearts have been scrubbed, but we can still get defiled from anything that accumulates—thoughts, movies, conversations, websites, and so on.

Our souls need to be cleansed from these kinds of things on a daily basis, in a regular trip to the dump. As with cleaning any stain, time is of the essence; the longer it sits the worse it gets. Otherwise the caked-on gunk hardens and calcifies.

This principle is sound when it comes to just about every area of life. In your finances: don't let the receipts get crazy; balance the books often. In your health: many do crash diets, P90X for a few months, then nothing; better to do a little every day. So it is with your soul: daily attention is the best way to roll. Robert Murray McCheyne, the great Scottish preacher, wrote, "I must never think a sin too small to need immediate application to the blood of Christ."

And don't rely on a weekly spiritual booster shot—going to church on Sunday to fill your tank so that you can coast the rest of the week. Stains will start to set in. Use a Tide pen approach.

Here are four ways to let Jesus daily spot clean your heart:

1. SPEND TIME WITH HIM IN HIS WORD.

Psalm 119:9 asks, "How can a young man cleanse his way? By taking heed according to Your word." When was the last time you opened your Bible?

A wise old man told a boy, "There are two wolves always fighting inside me. One is filled with anger, hate, jealousy, shame, and lies. The other wolf is filled with love, joy, truth, and peace. This battle rages inside of you and all men."

The boy thought for a moment and asked, "Which wolf will win?"

The old man answered, "The one you feed."

We need God's Word to give us fuel so that the right wolf rises and the wrong one starves.

2. PRAY AND TALK TO HIM THROUGHOUT THE DAY.

Ongoing dialogue through bursts of communication is a great way to keep in contact with your heavenly Father. You can honestly talk to him anywhere about anything. He's right there. Simply take off the mask. Stop the pretense. Stop hiding. Come clean. It feels so good to be forgiven, and it allows you to be authentically you: broken but loved, marred but chosen, heavy hearted but being healed. You can't be healthy and whole without unburdening your heart before the Lord.

3. LISTEN TO WORSHIP MUSIC AND PODCASTS.

We live in amazing technological times. Even when you're commuting you can experience digital discipleship. If you get into it, you'll be excited for traffic because you'll be able to finish a whole message or keep singing along with your favorite worship band.

4. SERVE AT YOUR CHURCH.

When you find a place in your local body of believers, you'll be more likely to stay on mission and fight off the lethargy that comes from sitting around too much. It will also keep you from being a consumer at your church and turn you into a contributor.

Each one of these strategies will help you keep the garage of your heart uncluttered.

A Foundation You Can Build On

Recently, while watching an episode of *60 Minutes*, I was reminded of the importance of being anchored. The segment was about the 645-foot-tall Millennium Tower in San Francisco. Built out of reinforced concrete wrapped in glass at a cost of $550 million, the 58 stories are full of plush units that boast every amenity possible so as to attract the tech moguls of Silicon Valley and the venture capitalists that flock to the Bay area. Even 49ers quarterback legend Joe Montana bought a unit. The smallest two-bedroom units sold for millions.

YOU CAN'T
BE
HEALTHY
AND
WHOLE
★ WITHOUT ★
UNBURDENING
YOUR
HEART
BEFORE THE
LORD

When it opened, it was the tallest residential building west of the Mississippi. It won numerous awards, several of them simply for its sophisticated construction. It is amazing in every way. There is only one problem: the building is sinking. So far it's down by 17 inches. It's also tilting 14 inches to the northwest. Even as I type, it is slowly but surely being swallowed up by the earth at the rate of 1.5 to 2 inches a year.

To demonstrate the effect, some residents rolled a marble across the expensive hardwood floor in their condo. Mid-roll the marble stopped, turned around, and started rolling back the direction the building is tilting.

The city of San Francisco and its engineers asserted the building is safe, even in the event of an earthquake, but many are skeptical. People are selling their units, and losing millions—selling for half of what they bought in at.

So what's the problem? The foundation isn't anchored in bedrock. When it was built, engineers went down eighty feet deep into a layer of sand. But you have to go down at least two hundred feet, through layers of history going back to the 1906 earthquake and the gold rush, to reach bedrock. What can they do to fix it?

One of the solutions under consideration is to perpetually freeze the ground under the building to try to harden it. Another is to remove twenty stories from the top of the building to reduce its weight. Of course, the surest way is to somehow get it on piles of rock, but how do you drill under a skyscraper with a thousand people living inside? And who pays for all this?

The moral of the story is that if you want to go up high and be able to withstand the stress of life you need to build your slab on something solid. Of course, that's exactly what Jesus said in one of his more famous parables:

> "These words I speak to you are not incidental additions to your life, homeowner improvements to your standard of living. They are foundational words, words to build a life on. If you work these words into your life, you are like a smart carpenter who built his house on solid rock. Rain poured down, the river flooded, a tornado hit—but nothing moved that house. It was fixed to the rock.
>
> "But if you just use my words in Bible studies and don't work them into your life, you are like a stupid carpenter who built his house on the sandy beach. When a storm rolled in and the waves came up, it collapsed like a house of cards." (Matthew 7:24–27 THE MESSAGE)

It's important to keep bringing all that accumulates in your life to the Lord. You can even make taking out the actual trash in your house a spiritual exercise; every time you grab a bag and head for the garbage cans, run through a checklist about what needs to get tossed out in your soul:

- Are you feeling heavy hearted?
- Do you feel left out?
- Are you discouraged?
- What are you suppressing or feeling guilty about?
- What has your alter ego been up to lately?
- What are you scared about?

Get rid of it by giving it all to God, and you will be synced up and primed to receive the phantom power he wants to give you.

Now, if you'll excuse me, I have coffee to make and a cardboard box to deal with.

Conclusion

THE ACE OF SPADES

*I must study Politicks and War that my sons
may have liberty to study Mathematicks and
Philosophy. My sons ought to study Mathematicks
and Philosophy, Geography, natural History,
Naval Architecture, navigation, Commerce and
Agriculture, in order to give their Children a right
to study Painting, Poetry, Musick, Architecture,
Statuary, Tapestry, and Porcelaine.*

—John Adams

There was once an imposing statue of King George III
in the heart of New York City. It's hard to imagine
such a thing now, but when we were a part of the British
empire, the statue was placed prominently in the heart of
Manhattan, and its meaning was inescapable. We were subjects of the king. A detailed description tells us just what it
looked like:

The monarch is nine feet tall and made of lead and gold, sitting atop a proportionally large horse. A fifteen-foot-high marble pedestal supports the two. Modeling it after an Italian statue of Roman emperor Marcus Aurelius, sculptor Joseph Wilton desired that it might "metaphorically assume and actually aspire to the wisdom and grandeur of the ancient stoic leader and thinker."

The statue sat right outside where George Washington placed his headquarters at the start of the Revolutionary War. He had moved the Continental Congress to New York after the colonists managed to drive the British out of Boston. He hoped to be able to maintain control of the city, but he was unable to do so, and the British would control New York for most of the war.

During this short-lived occupation, the city was greatly divided. Loyalists devoted to the Crown reported Washington's movements and artillery placements to the British. Some of them feared that the statue would be tampered with, so they placed a black wrought-iron fence around it to protect it.

The Declaration of Independence, written by Thomas Jefferson and signed by the Continental Congress, was read throughout the colonies. Its message quickly ricocheted around the world. General Washington assembled his armies and had the document read aloud to them. Afterward, a great celebration broke out, and a mob of drunken, wild soldiers and patriot citizens stormed down Broadway to tear down the statue of the king.

Historian David McCullough described the scene: "With ropes and bars, they pulled down the gilded lead statue of

George III on his colossal horse. In their fury the crowd hacked off the sovereign's head, severed the nose, clipped the laurels that wreathed the head, and mounted what remained of the head on a spike outside a tavern." King George III was unceremoniously and unmistakably dethroned.

This momentous scene captures the end of a power struggle and the rightful removal of the vestiges of former authority. The monarch's statue symbolized who was in control. So it is with your heart: whoever or whatever sits on the throne of your heart is what controls your life.

Idol Thoughts

Ultimately the war we have been talking about throughout this book is the quest to eliminate idolatry. At the end of the day, all of our problems are worship problems. Our love of attention makes us value other people more than we value Jesus. Our love of stuff means we worship possessions more than Jesus. Our struggles with boldness cause us to worship comfort more than Jesus. And on and on it goes.

The good news is that since worship gets you in this mess, worship can get you out. To win the battle, we must tear down the things that have been erected where only God belongs, in the preeminent place of honor, value, and glory. It is a daily battle to continue to put God on the throne and banish the would-be kings, but it's also the only way to get out of your own way, to stop sabotaging yourself, and to lay hold of victory.

You might have seen images of marines in Vietnam with ace of spades playing cards in their helmets. US troops heard that Viet Cong soldiers were superstitious about the spade symbol and saw it as a bad omen to encounter it by chance. So it became common practice to leave an ace of spades on the bodies of killed Vietnamese and even to litter the forested grounds and fields with the card in an attempt to spook them and avoid a firefight. Some soldiers even wrote the United States Playing Card Company and requested modified decks containing nothing but the ace of spades so they could use them in their psychological warfare. Worship doesn't just win the war—worship is the war. It's the ace of spades.

Idols promise freedom but bring bondage. They tell us we will be autonomous but leave us cowering in fear like Adam and Eve after they took the forbidden fruit. As you battle against the things that would elevate themselves over Jesus, you tap into the true boldness of authentic worship. And when you are authentically yourself and walk humbly as a follower of Jesus, you can live in confidence without fear, distraction, depression, anxiety, worry, regret, quarrels, addictions, darkness, selfishness, self-sabotage, narcissism, the held-hostage version of yourself you don't want to be, or anything else that gets in your way and stunts your growth. Draw a line in the sand—a crimson line painted with the blood of Jesus—and decide that the cycle ends with you. Your children don't have to inherit from you what you inherited from your parents. Give yourself to war so that they won't have to.

Hear these empowering words that David wrote in Psalm 91:

> He who dwells in the secret place of the Most High
> Shall abide under the shadow of the Almighty.

WORSHIP
DOESN'T
JUST WIN THE
WAR

WORSHIP
IS THE
WAR

> I will say of the Lord, "He is my refuge and my fortress;
> My God, in Him I will trust." . . .
>
> You shall not be afraid of the terror by night,
> Nor of the arrow that flies by day,
> Nor of the pestilence that walks in darkness,
> Nor of the destruction that lays waste at noonday.
>
> A thousand may fall at your side,
> And ten thousand at your right hand;
> But it shall not come near you. . . .
> Because you have made the Lord, who is my refuge,
> Even the Most High, your dwelling place. (Psalm 91:1–9)

Did you catch that? God promises that if you make him your God, you don't have to be afraid of terror by night! As someone who has struggled with fear my whole life, this is wonderfully freeing. Scary thoughts and bad dreams have been a problem for me all my days. The "terror by night" David talks about has been a great source of anxiety and has stolen so much peace. But if I "abide under the shadow of the Almighty"—put nothing above God in my heart—then the terror by night cannot touch me.

THREE LAWS OF THE JUNGLE

The more I have learned to tear down the impostors in my heart and prepare the way in my spirit for the Lord, the greater peace I have experienced. But even on my best days my fear hasn't fully gone away—and I don't expect it to until I get to heaven. How does that jibe with God's promise in Psalm 91?

Don't miss this, because it is a huge distinction: *just because you don't have to fear evil doesn't mean you'll never feel afraid*. Protection isn't the same as exemption. And what's promised to you is not exemption from attack, in which you will never walk through bad days or nightmares, but rather protection against whatever may come your way. Following Jesus doesn't put you in a luxury box seat, watching things play out far above the action while you comfortably sip champagne and eat finger foods. You are going to be in the thick of it, your face marred by dust and sweat and grime as you charge headlong into action, knowing God both goes before you and stands as your rear guard.

Your nostrils will be filled with smoke and the coppery smell of blood as your unseen enemies get close enough to make you feel like you're in danger. The spiritual support God provides is not an ivory tower of exemption or a HEPA-filtered clean room or a hermetically sealed bubble suit; it is a living and active phalanx of protection in a high-stakes combat situation. Following God means being on the front lines of a battle and knowing he's got your back and is watching your six.

We can see how this played out in Jesus' life. God brought him safely through the battles he faced—including death—but that didn't mean he was never attacked. Quite the contrary; he was regularly opposed by enemies. In fact, his public ministry was bookended by two extreme episodes: the temptation in the wilderness and his suffering in the Garden of Gethsemane.

Mark wrote of Jesus' temptation: "Immediately the Spirit drove Him into the wilderness. And He was there in the wilderness forty days, tempted by Satan, and was with the wild beasts; and the angels ministered to Him" (1:12–13). Over a period that amounts to nearly six weeks, Satan tempted Jesus *constantly*, waging a nonstop spiritual battle that continued around the clock. During these days of terror in the wilderness, awful thoughts went through Jesus' head: *You should worship Satan. You should throw yourself off this building. You should give up on dying on the cross. And* (this is how I know the incarnation was legit and Jesus was totally human) *you should ditch your diet and eat carbs!*

These kinds of thoughts steal peace and cause terror. (And interestingly enough, they are close to the types of scary things I have had in my mind when I should have been sleeping.) Had Jesus given in to them, it would have taken him off the track God intended for his life.

Near the end of his ministry, Jesus experienced deep despair in the Garden of Gethsemane: "He plunged into a sinkhole of dreadful agony" (Mark 14:33 THE MESSAGE). He was so crushed by his thoughts, by this whole final scene, that capillaries under his skin began to burst, and blood began to go into his sweat glands.

What did Jesus do in those situations—when he needed to cross the barbed wire and rise from his knees with the wolf in his heart? Three keys emerge from those two stories.

First, every time the devil attacked Jesus in the desert, he responded by quoting God's Word. He confronted lies with truth, saying, "It is written, it is written, it is written." These words were his weapons of protection. It is significant that the record of this interaction doesn't say he pulled out Scripture and looked up a verse. He had these words committed to memory.

Setting God's Word before you like a sentry guarding a citadel allows you to defend your borders proactively.

Filling your heart with truth causes it to be inhospitable to terror. When it is soaked in praise and steeped in Scripture, the enemy cannot gain traction. The living water and the oil of God's Holy Spirit will cause the enemy's weapons to glance right off.

If you leave food out, it will attract bugs. What are you leaving out that attracts worry and fear? If you're allowing negative thoughts, if you're allowing grumbling, if you're cynical, if you're gossipy, if you have a glass-is-half-empty mentality, if you're selfish, if you're proud—all of these things are the works of the flesh. Terror grabs ahold of this stuff, and it will never be satisfied.

Ditch the things terror thrives on. Starve that fear wolf, and feed your spirit. Scripture shores up the perimeter and gives the enemy nothing to eat.

Second, when Jesus was in the grips of the terror by night, he told God what he was afraid of. He got on his knees and told his Father, *I'm afraid of the mission you gave me. I know you want me to do it, but I'm terrified of it. Could you get someone else? Could you find some other way?*

He named his fear—and as he verbalized it, he distanced himself from it. The enemy wants to isolate you in a loop of loneliness, going around and around and around in your mind. He hopes you will keep your fear a secret so he can smother you and suffocate you and steal your peace in silence. The moment you take that fear to God, everything changes. Bringing it to him shines light on it. You've forced the fear to the feet of the Father, where it has no choice but to look up at him in terror.

Will what you are afraid of go away? Sometimes it will. Maybe you'll pray, and boom! Instant miracle. In Jesus' case, God didn't change his plan, but Jesus was able to face the cross with God's help. That's the way to pray—tell God your fear but use a tone that says, "not my will, but yours be done" (Luke 22:42 NIV).

Finally, Jesus woke up his friends. He walked the ten paces to where the disciples were sleeping and said, in effect, "Hey, Peter, James, John,—I'm scared right now and really alone. It would mean a lot for you to be with me in this moment. I have been praying, but could you maybe say a little prayer for me too?" (Matthew 26:36–41, author's paraphrase). Jesus obviously understood the power of the wolf pack.

Do you know how much strength comes from getting people to pray for you? As kids, we had the sense to wake our parents up when we had nightmares. But somewhere along the journey, we stopped telling others we are afraid. If the Son of God knew to wake up a couple of buddies and ask them to pray for him, why are you living a nightmare that you're not telling anyone about? Are you allowing the bottom to drop out because you don't have the people who would wake up to pray if they knew what was going on?

Having people like that around you can literally save your life. A study found that experiencing three or more incidents of intense stress within a year (serious financial trouble, being fired, a divorce, etc.) triples the death rate in socially isolated middle aged men, but has no impact on the death rate of men who have many close relationships. As Rudyard Kipling wrote, "The strength of the Pack is the Wolf, and the strength of the Wolf is the Pack."

I experienced the life-or-death power of friendship much earlier in life than middle age. When I was a freshman and had just given my life to Jesus, there was a period so dark that I was sick to my stomach with thoughts of self-harm. It wasn't that I *wanted* to kill myself; I just had thoughts that told me I was *going* to.

One night when I was home alone, I couldn't shake the thought: *You're going to kill yourself. You're going to kill yourself. You're going to kill yourself.* And I tried to pray, tried to ask God to help me. Finally, I called one of my youth group leaders and told her what was going on.

"I feel like a dark force is smothering me with thoughts about death at my own hands, and I don't know what to do. I'm terrified right now, like the enemy is just going to chew me up." I began to sob. So many times I had wanted to tell someone but felt like I couldn't or that it was admitting I had done something wrong. Sharing those fears with another person was the most wonderfully relieving thing ever.

The leader immediately sensed that I was under spiritual attack, and she spoke words overflowing with life about me and my future and prayed for me. Then she gave two scriptures to me and told me to memorize and repeat them over and over again whenever those kind of thoughts surfaced:

> "You will keep him in perfect peace
> whose mind is stayed on You,
> because he trusts in You." (Isaiah 26:3)

> "I call heaven and earth as witnesses today against you, that
> I have set before you life and death, blessing and cursing;

therefore choose life, that both you and your descendants may live; that you may love the LORD your God, that you may obey His voice, and that you may cling to Him, for He is your life and the length of your days; and that you may dwell in the land which the Lord swore to your fathers, to Abraham, Isaac, and Jacob, to give them." (Deuteronomy 30:19–20)

Giving me those verses was like giving a lifeline to a drowning man. For years, they were my go-to defense when under heavy attack.

Around that time I also discovered how to use worship to control the atmosphere around me. I discovered I couldn't go to sleep without listening to a song by Delirious?: "What a Friend I've Found" from their *Live & In the Can* album. I would put this track on repeat on my boom box and turn the words of the Scriptures over in my mind. My youngest daughter, Clover, struggles with nightmares these days, and she has found comfort by singing "Tremble" by Mosaic MSC to herself while snuggling her black blankie.

Thoughts can't be erased; they have to be replaced. You have to create a new track to your life's soundtrack and let that be praise. Let that be worship. Let that be faith, not fear—because fear is faith in the enemy.

Now that I know what to do the moment intrusive thoughts begin, they haven't been so intense. Here and there I have fear flare ups, often at pivotal moments when God is about to do something great. My anxiety was extreme the week before my daughter Lenya went to heaven—I think because many people were about to come to know Jesus through the ways God would turn up the volume of our lives through the microphone called pain. It also ramped up intensely in the few weeks before we opened a Fresh Life campus in Salt Lake City. I remember it also being really bad in 2017 when I flew to Atlanta to speak to college students from all over the country at the Passion conference at the Georgia Dome.

My wife is my ride-or-die gangster for life. I wake her up when I am afraid and she does the same to me. We never let each other suffer alone. Wolves are known to intentionally regurgitate elk or deer or whatever they have killed in order to feed old, young, or injured members of the pack who can't get out to the hunt themselves. It is crucial that you let people know you are hurting so they can be strong where you are weak.

Use Scripture; tell God about your fear; wake people up. Those are the three things modeled for us by Jesus. They have saved my life, and they can do the same for you.

The Best Defense Is a Good Offense

Defending against evil is so important, but when dark times come, you must not forget to retaliate appropriately.

I have written this whole book as an excuse to tell you this: when the devil messes with you, it's a mistake on his part. Because every time he fights against something, he's tipping his hand so you can see what matters to him.

The only reason the enemy would come against you is because he sees value in you. The only reason he would try to force you to think something like *I'm worthless* or *No one wants me on their team* or *I'm never going to win* or *I stink*

USE
SCRIPTURE

*

TELL GOD
ABOUT YOUR
FEAR

*

WAKE
PEOPLE
UP

is because *it's not true*, and he wants to throw you off the trail of your God-given greatness.

It's because you're precious that he tries to make you feel worthless. It's because you're meant to choose life that he would try and suggest you should choose death. Whatever he says, it's the opposite, because he's a liar. Jesus knew this. *If Satan tells me to throw myself off the temple, I'm not going to do it. If he tells me to fall at his feet and worship him and not go to the cross, then I'm going to get up and go to the cross. I'm going to "set My face like a flint" toward Jerusalem* (Isaiah 50:7).

If Satan tells me he's going to give me everything in a moment so I can have instant gratification and not wait for God to give me what he wants to give me, I'm not going to listen. If he tells me to take a shortcut, I'm going to take the hard road instead.

The devil opposes what he's afraid of. So let your fear help you sniff out what he's trying to snuff out. Let it be a diagnostic tool to determine your calling.

Rise up and do exactly what the devil doesn't want you to do. Refuse to go gently into the night. Don't be taken without a fight. In jujitsu you use your opponent's force and energy against him. Likewise, when you experience terror during the darkness, become a source of terror to the kingdom of darkness. It's terror-jitsu.

I have literally said out loud, "It seems the enemy doesn't want us to do this. We must be on to something. So we'll not only do that, but we will also do this other thing too."

You're chosen. You're loved. You're called. You're equipped. You're a part of the spiritual lineage of Abraham and Isaac and Jacob. You're meant to dwell in the land and feed on his faithfulness. You're meant to show life to people who are hurting.

You're meant to encourage those who are weary and give the bread of life to those who are hungry. You are meant to pioneer and create and lead and design and invent and sing and dance and write. You will fall and get back up again, and learn from your mistakes, and grow wise and strong and brave. When your time here on earth is done, you are meant to leave a legacy that will ring out through the ages and touch thousands into eternity.

When the enemy tries to come at you to smother you, rise up in faith and do whatever he's trying to get you not to do with twice as much resolve and ten times the determination, relying on the power of the Holy Spirit. When you're full of anxious thoughts and worry and spiritual warfare and peer pressure from the world, and your mind feels as though there are squirrels running around inside it, don't back down; double down. There are people in your peripheral vision who need to be noticed, and if you pay attention to them instead of wanting the world to pay attention to you, you'll tap into things God put inside you that are being neglected. When the Americans tore down the massive statue of King George in Manhattan, they had their fun with it as they celebrated their newly declared independence. Since it didn't belong to them it was only right that it be returned to the British, so that's exactly what they did—by melting it down, fashioning the lead into bullets, and returning it one musket ball at a time.

Don't just discard the strongholds and idols that Jesus gives you the power to wage war on. Melt down what has been torn down and turn it into ammunition so you can fire it across enemy lines.

I must admit I am a little misty-eyed knowing our time together is over, and as I hand you your helmet (with an ace of spades tucked in it for good luck), I want you to know how much I have enjoyed sharing all this with you. I came across the barbed wire to get this intel to you, and now you need to cross it too. The book is over, but your mission has just begun. I can't fight this battle for you, but I'll be here anytime you need to pull this book out and go over it again. This is a journey you must be willing to take for yourself. I believe in you—the version of yourself you were born to be. You can do this. It won't be easy or fast or pain free, but you *can* do this.

One last quick piece of advice before you go: A boxing instructor once explained the difference between a *cross* (in which you hit hard with a straight punch) and a *jab* (in which you throw a fast, light punch that is more distracting than damaging). She said something that I think will put you in the right mind-set as you rise up as the nurturing warrior wolf you were born to be: "The jab keeps them busy, but the cross is your power."

THE
JAB
KEEPS THEM
BUSY
BUT THE
CROSS
IS YOUR
POWER

Acknowledgments

Famed astronaut John Glenn once said, "I went to the moon but 400,000 supported at NASA so we all went to the moon." That is very much how I feel about this book. Yes, I was the one in the nonprescription Warby Parker frames, staring at the computer keys trying not to succumb to the paralysis by analysis that sets in when you overthink things. But my supporting cast is lengthy, and for that I am exceedingly and overwhelmingly grateful. We all went to the moon.

I began nearly every writing session in this book by playing Kanye West's *808s and Heartbreak*. It became the bell that told my lizard brain to take a hike so the me I am often afraid to be could take the wheel. Thank you, Kanye, for a truly incredible record.

Thank you, Lysa TerKeurst and your incredible crew, for the invaluable feedback on the manuscript and all the golden wisdom you guys have so generously imparted to our team. Fleah was pretty much the worst, but we love the rest of you like crazy. This book straight up got better because of our time with you, and that is a fact.

Thank you specifically to everyone at Fresh Life who has been hands-on with this project— Alie, Amanda, Chelsea, Elisha, Katelyn, Mckenzie—but in a larger sense, thank you to the whole Fresh Life staff and impact team for being in the trenches with us. What a life we get to live, what a Savior we get to serve.

Thank you, Austin, for being a friend and a truly wonderful agent. You have believed in this book from the beginning and been such a loyal, steady, and consistent ally in this insanely special publishing adventure, and I appreciate you.

Thank you, Meaghan, for another ace editing job. The words that aren't in this book make the ones that are even stronger. You did kill some of my darlings as the overgrown, 70,000-plus-word manuscript transformed into the svelte, compact shape it is in today, but thank you for standing up for the reader—as Jennie put it, "Someone's got to."

Thank you, Debbie and the whole W team, for your spirit, passion, and continued belief in my writing. Thank you for always taking it personally. Kristi, you can be an honorary Fresh Life employee anytime you want. Daisy, we still have never met face to face; if you are a real person, then thank you too. If not, please disregard. Either way, from email you seem super kind, so if you are not real, that is even more impressive.

Most all thank you Jennie, Alivia, Lenya, Daisy, Clover, and Lennox—you are my people. You have also had more encounters with Evilevi, aka the me I don't want to be, than anyone and, amazingly, you still put up with me. I'll never understand it. But I love you. Where you are home is. Thank you for putting up with the glazed and foggy look on my face when you try to talk to me when I am writing. Tabasco, thank you for hanging with me during early morning writing sessions.

Thank you, Jesus, for being the King of my heart and trumping every card my flesh, the devil, and the world can throw at me. Thank you for calling a ratboy your treasure and giving me a future and a hope. It is an honor to be trusted with your phantom power and the privilege of carrying this message.

APPENDIX A

SCRIPTURE TO MEMORIZE

Here are some incredible passages to focus on when you need to evict troublesome thoughts. Each will fill your mind with peace and force out the thoughts you are trying to remove in the same way that pouring water into a pitcher forces out all the air.

> Let love be without hypocrisy. Abhor what is evil. Cling to what is good. Be kindly affectionate to one another with brotherly love, in honor giving preference to one another; not lagging in diligence, fervent in spirit, serving the Lord; rejoicing in hope, patient in tribulation, continuing steadfastly in prayer. (Romans 12:9–12)

> Love never gives up.
> Love cares more for others than for self.
> Love doesn't want what it doesn't have.
> Love doesn't strut,
> Doesn't have a swelled head,
> Doesn't force itself on others,

Isn't always "me first,"
Doesn't fly off the handle,
Doesn't keep score of the sins of others,
Doesn't revel when others grovel,
Takes pleasure in the flowering of truth,
Puts up with anything,
Trusts God always,
Always looks for the best,
Never looks back,
But keeps going to the end. (1 Corinthians 13:4–7
THE MESSAGE)

But the fruit the Holy Spirit produces is love, joy and peace. It is being patient, kind and good. It is being faithful and gentle and having control of oneself. There is no law against things of that kind. Those who belong to Christ Jesus have nailed their sinful desires to his cross. They don't want these things anymore. (Galatians 5:22–24 NIrv)

For where envy and self-seeking exist, confusion and every evil thing are there. But the wisdom that is from above is first pure, then peaceable, gentle, willing to yield, full of mercy and good fruits, without partiality and without hypocrisy. Now the fruit of righteousness is sown in peace by those who make peace. (James 3:16–18)

O God, You are my God;
Early will I seek You;
My soul thirsts for You;

My flesh longs for You
In a dry and thirsty land
Where there is no water.
So I have looked for You in the sanctuary,
To see Your power and Your glory.

Because Your lovingkindness is better than life,
My lips shall praise You.
Thus I will bless You while I live;
I will lift up my hands in Your name.
My soul shall be satisfied as with marrow and fatness,
And my mouth shall praise You with joyful lips.

When I remember You on my bed,
I meditate on You in the night watches.
Because You have been my help,
Therefore in the shadow of Your wings I will rejoice.
My soul follows close behind You;
Your right hand upholds me. (Psalm 63:1–8)

But also for this very reason, giving all diligence, add
to your faith virtue, to virtue knowledge, to knowledge
self-control, to self-control perseverance, to perseverance godliness, to godliness brotherly kindness, and to
brotherly kindness love. For if these things are yours
and abound, you will be neither barren nor unfruitful in
the knowledge of our Lord Jesus Christ. (2 Peter 1:5–8)

Finally, be strong in the Lord and in his mighty power.
Put on the full armor of God, so that you can take

your stand against the devil's schemes. For our struggle is not against flesh and blood, but against the rulers, against the authorities, against the powers of this dark world and against the spiritual forces of evil in the heavenly realms. Therefore put on the full armor of God, so that when the day of evil comes, you may be able to stand your ground, and after you have done everything, to stand. Stand firm then, with the belt of truth buckled around your waist, with the breastplate of righteousness in place, and with your feet fitted with the readiness that comes from the gospel of peace. In addition to all this, take up the shield of faith, with which you can extinguish all the flaming arrows of the evil one. Take the helmet of salvation and the sword of the Spirit, which is the word of God.

And pray in the Spirit on all occasions with all kinds of prayers and requests. With this in mind, be alert and always keep on praying for all the Lord's people. (Ephesians 6:10–18 NIV)

For your obedience has become known to all. Therefore I am glad on your behalf; but I want you to be wise in what is good, and simple concerning evil. And the God of peace will crush Satan under your feet shortly.

The grace of our Lord Jesus Christ be with you. Amen. (Romans 16:19–20)

Since Jesus died and broke loose from the grave, God will most certainly bring back to life those who died in Jesus.

And then this: We can tell you with complete confidence—we have the Master's word on it—that when the Master comes again to get us, those of us who are still alive will not get a jump on the dead and leave them behind. In actual fact, they'll be ahead of us. The Master himself will give the command. Archangel thunder! God's trumpet blast! He'll come down from heaven and the dead in Christ will rise—they'll go first. Then the rest of us who are still alive at the time will be caught up with them into the clouds to meet the Master. Oh, we'll be walking on air! And then there will be one huge family reunion with the Master. So reassure one another with these words. (1 Thessalonians 4:14–18 THE MESSAGE)

> The LORD is my shepherd;
> I shall not want.
> He makes me to lie down in green pastures;
> He leads me beside the still waters.
> He restores my soul;
> He leads me in the paths of righteousness
> For His name's sake.
>
> Yea, though I walk through the valley of the shadow
>   of death,
> I will fear no evil;
> For You are with me;
> Your rod and Your staff, they comfort me.
>
> You prepare a table before me in the presence of
>   my enemies;

You anoint my head with oil;
My cup runs over.
Surely goodness and mercy shall follow me
All the days of my life;
And I will dwell in the house of the LORD
Forever. (Psalm 23:1–6)

"Let not your heart be troubled; you believe in God, believe also in Me. In My Father's house are many mansions; if it were not so, I would have told you. I go to prepare a place for you. And if I go and prepare a place for you, I will come again and receive you to Myself; that where I am, there you may be also. And where I go you know, and the way you know." (John 14:1–4)

Appendix B

COMPENDIUM OF USELESS TIDBITS

Whether you are making conversation at a cocktail party or trying to win *Jeopardy* or HQ, these tips and tidbits are sure to help. Even more, they are a fun reminder of all the things we have covered.

- Wolf Facts
  - Wolves are susceptible to contagious yawning, which is believed to be linked to empathy.
  - While wolves are apex predators, they exhibit the rare behaviors of adopting orphaned wolf pups and holding a place in their society for elders.
  - Wolves are known to regurgitate whatever they have killed to feed old, young, or injured members of the pack who cannot hunt for themselves.
- Space Facts
  - The International Space Station (ISS) travels 17,500 miles an hour, or 5 miles per second.
  - The ISS is 200 to 250 miles away from the Earth's surface.

- Astronauts on the ISS watch sixteen sunrises and sunsets in one day through the window of the Cupola module.
- A space shuttle uses more fuel taking off than the rest of the flight combined.
- People have on average five hundred intrusive thoughts within a sixteen-hour day, each lasting an average of fourteen seconds.
- The largest living species of lizard on Earth, the Komodo dragon, is able to kill pigs and cows with their venom.
- Steve Jobs's last words were, "Oh wow. Oh wow. Oh wow."
- It takes seventy-two different muscles to produce speech.
- On average you speak 16,000 words per day, which adds up to a whopping 860.3 million words in a lifetime.
- Because of a bet with his editor, Dr. Seuss wrote *Green Eggs and Ham* with only fifty different words.
- Crowd noise in a stadium has a verifiable impact on the game; for every ten thousand fans present, a home team gains an additional 0.1 goal advantage.
- Facts From *Everyday Emotional Intelligence*
  - Being the recipient of rudeness reduces creativity by 30 percent and originality by 25 percent.
  - Those who observe poor behavior perform 20 percent worse on word puzzles than others.
  - Our range of emotional skills is relatively set by our midtwenties, and our accompanying behaviors are, by that time, deep-seated habits.
- When we hear a story, our bodies release cortisol, a stress hormone, that isn't flushed from our system until there is a resolution.

- Our brains recognize the beginning-middle-end structure of a story and reward us for clearing up any ambiguity. We earn a dopamine reward every time our brains help us understand something in our world—even if that explanation is incomplete or wrong.
- Social Media Facts
  - Americans spend up to 5 hours a day on their phones, which add up to 150 hours a month and approximately 14 years over the course of a lifetime.
  - We get the same dopamine response from "likes," texts, notifications, and emails as we do from gambling.
  - Experts admit to such practices as holding back likes until a time when the algorithms indicate you are most likely to spend a good period of time on the device.
- About 45 percent of our actions each day are habits.
- Thomas Jefferson Facts
  - He was a lawyer, surveyor, ardent meteorologist, botanist, agronomist, archaeologist, paleontologist, Native American ethnologist, classicist, and brilliant architect.
  - He wrote the Declaration of Independence at age thirty-three.
- Those who commit their goals to paper are 42 percent more likely to accomplish them and earn nine times as much over their lifetimes as people who don't.
- Hans van Leeuwen, a physicist, discovered that every time a domino falls, it generates a force sufficient to knock down a domino twice as big as itself.
- The world record for number of folds to a piece of paper is twelve.

- Twenty percent of all oxygen you breathe goes to the brain.
- When your heart is beating at approximately 120 beats per minute, you will not be nearly as sharp-witted. At 150 BPM, your mind shuts down.
- Nervous energy usually causes you to hunch over, tuck your chin, put your hands on your neck, or cross your arms. This elicits the release of the stress hormone cortisol into your system. However, putting your hands on your hips or in the air elicits your body to release testosterone and your cortisol levels can drop as much as 25 percent.
- Experiencing three or more incidents of intense stress within a year (e.g., serious financial trouble, being fired, or divorce) triples the death rate in socially isolated middle-aged men, but has no impact on the death rate of men who have many close relationships.

NOTES

INTRODUCTION

xv "To be prepared for war": "From George Washington to the United States Senate and House of Representatives, 8 January 1790," Founders Online, National Archives, last modified February 1, 2018, http://founders.archives.gov/documents /Washington/05-04-02-0361.

xx "power of joy in battle": Theodore Roosevelt, "A Colonial Survival," *The Cosmopolitan* 14 (November 1892–April 1893), 232.

xxii "became the most magnificent soldier": Edmund Morris, *The Rise of Theodore Roosevelt* (1979; repr. New York: Random House, 2001), 674.

xxii "The moment one definitely commits oneself": William Hutchison Murrary, *The Scotting Himalayan Expedition* (London: J. M. Dent, 1951), 7.

CHAPTER 1: THE WOLF YOU NEVER KNEW YOU WANTED TO BE

3 "I want to be alone": Paul Lester, "From the Bedroom to the Universe," *Melody Maker*, October 23, 1993, 29.

13 a wolf: John 10:12.

13 an angel of light: 2 Corinthians 11:14.

13 a serpent: Genesis 3; Revelation 12:9, 20:2.

13 a roaring lion: 1 Peter 5:8.

13 wise like serpents: Matthew 10:16.

14 susceptible to contagious yawning: Helen Thompson,

"Yawning Spreads Like a Plague in Wolves," Smithsonian.
com, August 27, 2014, https://www.smithsonianmag.com
/science-nature/yawning-spread-plague-wolves-180952484/.

14 **"They care for their pups"**: Jim and Jamie Dutcher, *The Wisdom of Wolves: Lessons from the Sawtooth Pack* (Washington, DC: National Geographic, 2018), 20–21.

CHAPTER 2: (+) OR (–)?

23 **"Hey, Mom, it's October 1 today"**: Julian Treasure, "How to Speak So That People Want to Listen," TEDGlobal 2013, Edinburgh, Scotland, June 2013, https://www.ted.com/talks /julian_treasure_how_to_speak_so_that_people_want_to_listen /transcript?language=en.

23 **"Billy's faith was more of a 'faith despite'"**: Hanspeter Nüesch, *Ruth and Billy Graham: The Legacy of a Couple* (Grand Rapids: Baker, 2014), 193.

24 **"Some people low-rate you"**: Nüesch, *Ruth and Billy Graham*, 194.

28 **"I'm glad that when God paints"**: Charles Swindoll, *Elijah: A Man of Heroism and Humility* (Nashville: Thomas Nelson, 2000), 111.

28 **"Before battle of fist"**: *Kung Fu Panda 3*, directed by Alessandro Carloni and Jennifer Yuh Nelson (20th Century Fox Home Entertainment, 2016), DVD.

29 **"You have enemies?"**: Victor Hugo, "Villemain" (1848), in *The Works of Victor Hugo*, vol. 14 (n.p.: Jenson Society, 1907), 67.

31 **"It was the best of times"**: Charles Dickens, *A Tale of Two Cities* (1859; repr. n.p.: Dover, 1999), 1.

32 **In the book *Extreme Ownership***: Jocko Willink and Leif Babin, *Extreme Ownership: How US Navy SEALs Lead and Win* (New York: St. Martin's Press, 2015), 199.

34 **"Would we know that the major chords were sweet"**: Anonymous, *New York Observer* 84, November 29, 1906, 713.

35 **more than two-thirds of Americans:** National Center for Health Statistics, *Health, United States, 2016: With Chartbook on Long-Term Trends in Health* (Hyattsville, MD, 2017), https://www.cdc.gov/nchs/data/hus/hus16.pdf#053.

35 **the most in-debt generation:** Brené Brown, "The Power of Vulnerability," TEDxHouston, Houston, TX, June 2010, https://www.ted.com/talks/brene_brown_on_vulnerability.

CHAPTER 3: TSA ON THE BRAIN

37 **"Perfection is finally attained":** Antoine de Saint Exupéry, *Terre des Hommes* (1939), trans. Lewis Galantière.

40 **"The mind is its own place":** John Milton, *Paradise Lost,* bk. 1, lines 233–34.

43 **"A study back in the 1980s":** Jena E. Pincott, "Wicked Thoughts," *Psychology Today*, September 1, 2015, https://www.psychologytoday.com/articles/201509/wicked-thoughts.

45 **"thoughts are like trains":** Kevin Gerald, *Mind Monsters: Conquering Fear, Worry, Guilt, and Other Negative Thoughts That Work Against You* (Lake Mary, FL: Charisma House, 2012), 5.

45 *choo-choo-choose you*: If you don't get the reference, please watch this: https://www.youtube.com/watch?v=eWuAIS7Vs_M.

47 **"Better a thousand times err":** Theodore Roosevelt, *Administration—Civil Service* (New York: Putnam, 1902), 146.

CHAPTER 4: THE SECRET TO A MISERABLE LIFE

49 **"How much larger your life would be":** G. K. Chesterton, *Orthodoxy*, in *G. K. Chesterton: Collected Works*, vol. 1 (San Francisco: Ignatius Press, 1986), 223.

52 **for most Americans middle school is the worst:** Samantha Zabell, "Sorry, Parents: Middle School Is Scientifically the Worst," *Real Simple*, January 25, 2016, https://www.realsimple.com/work-life/family/kids-parenting/middle-school-worst-age-study.

57 "The primary concern of the spiritual life": Eugene Peterson, *Leap Over a Wall: Earthy Spirituality for Everyday Christians* (San Francisco: HarperSanFrancisco, 1997), 99.

57 "We cannot selectively numb emotions": Brené Brown, *The Gifts of Imperfection: Let Go of Who You're Supposed to Be and Embrace Who You Are* (Center City, MN: Hazelden, 2010), 70.

59 "honesty is the soil": Donald Miller, *Scary Close: Dropping the Act and Finding True Intimacy* (Nashville: Nelson Books, 2014), 168.

59 "Oh! what a tangled web we weave": Walter Scott, *Marmion* (Cambridge: Riverside Press, 1896), canto 6, lines 532–33.

64 "God will not have his work": Ralph Waldo Emerson, *The Essay on Self-Reliance* (East Aurora, NY: Roycrofters, 1908), 11.

CHAPTER 5: MIND YOUR WORDS

72 "Well, the Jerk Store called": *Seinfeld,* season 8, episode 13, "The Comeback," directed by David Owen Trainor, written by Gregg Kavet and Andy Robin, featuring Jerry Seinfeld and Jason Alexander, aired January 30, 1997, on NBC.

73 Orville Wright was heartsick: Nsikan Akpan, "8 Things You Didn't Know About Orville Wright," *Science*, August 20, 2015, https://www.pbs.org/newshour/science/8-things-didnt -know-orville-wright.

79 "I only regret that I have but one life": David McCullough, *1776* (New York: Simon & Schuster, 2005), loc. 3568–3572, Kindle.

79 "Sergeant, the Spanish bullet": Mike Coppock, "Rough Ride: On San Juan Hill That July Morning, Disaster, Death, and Glory Were Just a Shot Away," *American History*, no. 6, 2018, 39.

79 "I see earth receding": Greg Laurie, *Finding Hope in the Last Words of Jesus* (Grand Rapids: Baker Books, 2009), 9.

79 "Oh wow": Mona Simpson, "A Sister's Eulogy for Steve Jobs," *New York Times*, October 30, 2011, https://www.nytimes.com /2011/10/30/opinion/mona-simpsons-eulogy-for-steve-jobs.html.

81 **72 different muscles to produce speech:** "Human Facts, ScienceFacts, http://www.science-facts.com/quick-facts/amazing -human-facts/.

81 **16,000 words:** Richard Knox, "Study: Men Talk Just as Much as Women," NPR, July 5, 2007, https://www.npr.org/templates /story/story.php?storyId=11762186.

81 **860.3 million in a lifetime:** Alexander Atkins, "How Many Words Does the Average Person Speak in a Lifetime?" Atkins Bookshelf, May 7, 2014, https://atkinsbookshelf.blog/tag/how -many-words-does-the-average-person-speak-in-their-lifetime/.

CHAPTER 6: IF YOU SAY SO

83 **"God's main business is blessing":** Eugene H. Peterson, *As Kingfishers Catch Fire: A Conversation on the Ways of God Formed by the Words of God* (Colorado Springs: Waterbrook, 2017), 47.

91 **"The doors of hell are locked":** C. S. Lewis, *The Problem of Pain* (1940; repr. New York: HarperCollins, 1996), 130.

94 **He wrote *The Cat in the Hat*:** Austin Kleon, *Steal Like an Artist: 10 Things Nobody Told You About Being Creative* (New York: Workman, 2012), 138.

95 **A researcher from Harvard University:** "Study Reveals Referees' Home Bias," *BBC News*, May 6, 2007, http://news.bbc.co.uk/2 /hi/uk_news/england/6629397.stm.

95 **"There can be no preaching":** William Barclay, *The Gospel of Mark*, rev. ed. (Philadelphia: Westminster, 1975), 140.

CHAPTER 7: BEING RUDE IS NOT CHEAP

99 **"If you want to gather honey":** Dale Carnegie, *How to Win Friends and Influence People* (1936; repr. New York: Pocket, 1998), 3.

99 **"Participants who were treated rudely":** Christine Porath and Christine Pearson, "The Price of Incivility: Lack of Respect

Hurts Morale—and the Bottom Line," in *Everyday Emotional Intelligence: Big Ideas and Practical Advice on How to Be Human at Work* (Cambridge: Harvard Business Review, 2018), eBook.

99 **"people who'd observed poor behavior":** Porath and Pearson, "The Price of Incivility."

104 **"Almost all research now indicates":** Gary Chapman, *Anger: Taming a Powerful Emotion* (1999; repr. Chicago: Moody, 2015), 86.

105 **"If you speak when angry":** Authorship of this saying cannot be definitively determined, but a likely author is Groucho Marx, who is reported to have given this advice to a contestant on a TV show. See "Speak When You're Angry and You'll Make the Best Speech You'll Ever Regret," Quote Investigator, May 17, 2014, https://quoteinvestigator.com/2014/05/17/angry-speech/.

107 **"One day the Wind and the Sun":** Æsop, *Fables,* retold by Joseph Jacobs, vol. 17, part 1, Harvard Classics (New York: P.F. Collier & Son, 1909–14); Bartleby.com, 2001. www.bartleby.com/17/1/.

108 **"If we are going to be true to ourselves":** Lysa TerKeurst, *It's Not Supposed to Be This Way: Finding Unexpected Strength When Disappointments Leave You Shattered* (Nashville: Nelson, 2018), 165.

112 **"If there is any secret of success":** Henry Ford, "How I Made a Success of My Business," *System,* November 1916.

112 **when we hear a story:** Brené Brown, *Rising Strong: How the Ability to Reset Transforms the Way We Live, Love, Parent, and Lead* (New York: Random House, 2015), 6.

112 **"In the absence of data":** Brown, *Rising Strong,* 79–80.

CHAPTER 8: TAKE BACK THE CONTROLS

119 **"R2, get us off this autopilot!":** *Star Wars: Episode 1—The Phantom Menace,* directed by George Lucas (1999; 20th Century Fox Home Entertainment, 2005), DVD.

119 **"We are what we repeatedly do"**: Will Durant, *The Story of Philosophy: The Lives and Opinions of the World's Greatest Philosophers from Plato to John Dewey* (1926; repr. New York: Pocket, 1953), 76.

121 **"OK, Google"**: These are the answers Alexa gave me at the time I wrote this book.

122 **"research suggests that our range of emotional skills"**: Daniel Goleman, Richard Boyatzis, and Annie McKee, "Primal Leadership: The Hidden Driver of Great Performance," in *Everyday Emotional Intelligence: Big Ideas and Practical Advice on How to Be Human at Work* (Cambridge: Harvard Business Review, 2018), eBook.

123 **According to research from Duke University**: David T. Neal, Wendy Wood, and Jeffrey M. Quinn, "Habits—A Repeat Performance," *Current Directions in Psychological Science* 15, no. 4 (2006), 198.

125 **Americans spend up to five hours a day**: Sarah Perez, "US Consumers Now Spend 5 Hours per Day on Mobile Devices," TechCrunch, March 3, 2107, https://techcrunch.com/2017/03/03/u-s-consumers-now-spend-5-hours-per-day-on-mobile-devices/.

126 *60 Minutes* **ran a special**: Anderson Cooper, "Brain Hacking," *60 Minutes*, April 9, 2017, transcript available at https://www.cbsnews.com/news/brain-hacking-tech-insiders-60-minutes/.

126 **"bright dings of pseudo-pleasure"**: Paul Lewis, "'Our Minds Can Be Hijacked': The Tech Insiders Who Fear a Smartphone Dystopia," *Guardian*, October 6, 2017, https://www.theguardian.com/technology/2017/oct/05/smartphone-addiction-silicon-valley-dystopia.

128 **"He read seven languages"**: David McCullough, *The American Spirit: Who We Are and What We Stand For* (New York: Simon and Schuster), 27.

128 **"We hold these truths"**: Declaration of Independence, 1776.

129 **"Sometime, somewhere along the line"**: McCullough, *American Spirit*, 42.

129 **42 percent more likely to accomplish them:** Mary Morrissey, "The Power of Writing Down Your Goals and Dreams," *Huffington Post*, updated December 6, 2017, https://www .huffingtonpost.com/marymorrissey/the-power-of-writing -down_b_12002348.html.

129 **earn nine times as much:** Mark Milotay, *Practical Goal Setting: A Guide for Real People Who Want to Live Unreal Lives* (n.p.: CreateSpace, 2013), 5–6.

CHAPTER 9: START BEFORE YOU'RE READY

133 **The way to get started:** Dave Smith, *The Quotable Walt Disney* (New York: Disney Editions, 2001), 246.

134 **A physicist named Hans van Leeuwen:** Sean Treacy, "Dominoes: More Powerful Than You Think," *Inside Science*, January 30, 2013, https://www.insidescience.org/news/dominoes-more -powerful-you-think.

134 **I came across a fascinating legend:** Nikola Slavkovic, "A Piece of Paper as Big as the Universe!," June 10, 2014, YouTube video, 2:34, https://www.youtube.com/watch?time_continue =69&v=AAwabyyqWK0

136 **if you attempt to fold a single sheet:** *MythBusters*, "Underwater Car," season 5, episode 3, aired January 24, 2007 on Discovery Channel, featuring Tory Belleci and Kari Byron.

137 **if you could somehow hit 103 folds:** "How Many Times Can You Really Fold a Piece of Paper in Half?" Relatively Interesting, August 6, 2015, http://www.relativelyinteresting.com/how-many -times-can-you-really-fold-a-piece-of-paper-in-half/.

137 **"Good and evil both increase":** C. S. Lewis, *Mere Christianity* (1952; repr. New York: HarperOne, 2001), 133.

143 **"A man can be as great as he wants to be":** "Famous Quotes by Vince Lombardi," Vince Lombardi (website), http://www .vincelombardi.com/quotes.html.

143 **"Once a man has made a commitment":** "Famous Quotes."

143 **"The harder you work":** "Famous Quotes."

144 **"Whenever anyone makes an important change"**: Bernard Roth, *The Achievement Habit: Stop Wishing, Start Doing, and Take Command of Your Life* (New York: HarperCollins, 2015), 105.

144 **"If you can break a habit"**: Charles Duhigg, *The Power of Habit: Why We Do What We Do in Life and Business* (New York: Random House, 2012), 20, 62.

CHAPTER 10: THE GAME BEFORE THE GAME

151 **"Finally they told him to go ahead"**: Tom Wolfe, *The Right Stuff* (New York: Picador, 1979), 198.

157 **In his book *10-Minute Toughness***: Jason Selk, *10-Minute Toughness: The Mental Training Program for the Winning Before the Game Begins* (n.p.: McGraw-Hill, 2009), 23–24.

159 **Amy Cuddy's TED talk**: Amy Cuddy, "Your Body Language May Shape Who You Are," TEDGlobal 2012, Edinburgh, Scotland, June 2012, https://www.ted.com/talks/amy_cuddy _your_body_language_shapes_who_you_are?language=en.

160 **Researchers have found that people respond**: Sebastien Gendry, "Urban Myth: It Takes More Muscles to Frown Than to Smile," Laughter Online University, accessed April 24, 2018, http://www.laughteronlineuniversity.com/true-false -takes-43-muscles-frown-17-smile/.

160 **Seeing someone display facial expressions**: David E. Nielson, *The 9 Dimensions of Conscious Success: It's All About YOU!* (Shippensburg, PA: Sound Wisdom, 2018), 163.

161 **In a study in France**: Travis Bradberry and Jean Graves, *Emotional Intelligence 2.0* (San Diego: TalentSmart, 2009), 114–15.

CHAPTER 11: NEVER BRING A HORSE TO A TANK FIGHT

169 **"You shall receive power"**: Acts 1:8.

180 **"Satan trembles, when he sees"**: William Cowper, "What

Various Hindrances We Meet," *Olney Hymns* (London: W. Oliver, 1779), no. 60.

180 **the TV show *MythBusters* was originally called:** Gary Strauss and USA Today, "MythBusters Is the Stuff of Legends, Tall Tales," *ABC News*, January 20, 2008, https://abcnews.go.com /Technology/story?id=4160444&page=1.

CHAPTER 12: BUTTERFLIES AND EAGLES

183 **"Mistakes aren't a necessary evil":** Ed Catmull with Amy Wallace, *Creativity, Inc.: Overcoming the Unseen Forces That Stand in the Way of True Inspiration* (New York: Penguin, 2014), eBook.

186 **If there were only one prayer:** Charles Spurgeon, "The Superlative Excellence of the Holy Spirit," June 12, 1864.

186 **The church is weak today:** Charles Spurgeon, "Receiving the Holy Spirit," July 13, 1884, https://www.spurgeongems.org /vols28-30/chs1790.pdf.

CHAPTER 13: A TRIP TO THE DUMP

201 **"brimming with garbage":** Roberto A. Ferdman, "What Happens to a City When Its Street Cleaners Go on Strike," *Quartz*, November 13, 2013, https://qz.com/146902/what -happens-to-a-city-when-its-street-cleaners-go-on-strike/.

205 **"I must never think a sin too small":** Andrew A. Bonar, ed., *Memoir and Remains of the Rev. Robert Murrary McCheyne* (Philadelphia: Presbyterian Board of Education, 1844), 182.

206 **the 645-foot-tall Millennium Tower:** John Wertheim, "San Francisco's Leaning Tower of Lawsuits," *60 Minutes*, aired November 5, 2017, CBS, transcript available at https://www. cbsnews.com/news/san-franciscos-leaning-tower-of-lawsuits/.

CONCLUSION

211 **"I must study":** John Adams to Abigail Adams, May 12, 1780, electronic edition, *Adams Family Papers: An Electronic*

Archive, Massachusetts Historical Society, http://www.masshist .org/digitaladams/archive/doc?id=L17800512jasecond. The original spelling has been preserved.

212 **The monarch is nine feet tall:** Bill O'Reilly and Martin Dugard, *Killing England: The Brutal Struggle for American Independence* (New York: Henry Holt, 2017), 83.

212 **"With ropes and bars":** David McCullough, *1776* (New York: Simon and Schuster, 2005), 137.

213 **ace of spades playing cards in their helmets:** "Ace of Spades in the Vietnam War," posted by vlogger, November 14, 2013, http://www.military.com/video/operations-and-strategy /vietnam-war/ace-of-spades-in-vietnam-war/2838824484001.

220 **A study found that experiencing:** Daniel Goldman et al., *Harvard Business Review: On Emotional Intelligence* (Harvard Business Press, 2015).

220 **"The strength of the Pack":** Rudyard Kipling, *The Second Jungle Book* (Leipzig: Tauchnitz, 1897), 33.

ABOUT THE AUTHOR

LEVI LUSKO, author of the bestselling books *Through the Eyes of a Lion* and *Swipe Right*, is the lead pastor of Fresh Life Church in Montana, Wyoming, Oregon, and Utah. He and his wife, Jennie, have one son, Lennox, and four daughters: Alivia, Daisy, Clover, and Lenya, who is in heaven. Levi travels around the world speaking about Jesus.

New Video Study for Your Church or Small Group

Study Guide
9780310094876

DVD
9780310094913

If you've enjoyed this book, now you can go deeper with the companion video Bible study!

In this five-session study, Levi helps you apply the principles in *I Declare War* to your life. The study guide includes video notes, group discussion questions, and personal study and reflection materials for in-between sessions.

Available now at your favorite bookstore, or streaming video on StudyGateway.com.

THOMAS NELSON
Since 1798

ALSO AVAILABLE FROM
LEVI LUSKO

This can't be real.

These thoughts swim through my mind and try to strangle me. My heart is shattered into a thousand pieces, each shard jagged and razor sharp. The pain is surreal, deafening, and catastrophic. My eyes burn. I want to cry, but the tears won't come. I want to scream, but it won't help. I am afraid. But I'm not alone....

You must not rely on the naked eye. What you think you see is not all that is there. There are unseen things. Spiritual things. Eternal things. You must learn to see life through the eyes of a Lion. Doing so is to utilize the telescope of faith, which will not only allow you to perceive the invisible--it will give you the strength to do the impossible.

From the introduction of Levi Lusko's book, Through the Eyes of a Lion.

Through the Eyes of a Lion **will help you:**

Embrace the power of hope in a world that is often filled with suffering and loss.

Discover a manifesto for high-octane living when grief and despair are paralyzing.

Learn how to let your pain become your platform.

• • •

LeviLusko.com
Available wherever books and ebooks are sold.

Church and small group resources also available.

ALSO AVAILABLE FROM
LEVI LUSKO

God wants you to have amazing sex!

In case you haven't noticed, our generation has stripped sex of any emotional or spiritual significance, and now it's simply viewed as a physical source of pleasure and enjoyment. What most people don't know is that sex is a powerful thing that can be used to do great good or great damage. In fact, relationships are a matter of life-and-death importance.

Whether you're fed up with dating and hooking up as usual, tired of being single, numb because of porn and casual sex, or curious about how to improve your marriage, this book is for you.

In *Swipe Right*, Levi Lusko shares from his own life experiences and from God's Word on how to:

Regret-proof your marriage bed and your deathbed.

Learn how to avoid and treat sexual scars by careful living today.

Turn the clumsy "sex talk" with your child into dialogue that leads to wise choices.

Transform a stagnant marriage by trading predictable nearness for mind-blowing intimacy.

• • •

LeviLusko.com
Available wherever books and ebooks are sold.

Church and small group resources also available.